MILES FROM HOME

EVACUEES IN TIMBERSCOMBE
DURING THE SECOND WORLD WAR

ALAN HINES

https://alanhines.com

'When we moved back to London, they called us 'carrot crunchers'.

Eddie Gande

CONTENTS

WHAT THEY REMEMBER...

The man in Ye Olde Malthouse died this morning. Everyone knew Maurice Huxtable or knew who he was. He lived his entire 88 years in this little village. Huxtables have been in Timberscombe since the 1700s, and Maurice was the last.

The world went to war again when Maurice was eight. Large metropolitan areas were sure to be targets for German bombers, so the government evacuated children from London and other cities to rural villages where they would be safe for the duration of the war. Some of their mothers came, too. Two boys from the East End of London named Joe Farmer and Ronald Dedman were billeted with Maurice's mother and father. Instant older brothers to an only child. He told me his recollections of Joe and Ronnie and the other evacuees in the village. Memories came to him in fragments. But then the more he talked, the more the past came forward in his mind.

Young Maurice was slim and athletic, but by the end of his life, only a wisp of him was left. He wasn't known to be good-natured. Obstinate came to mind first. He had been a stern and distant father, as his father Dudley had been with him. His lifelong passion was mastering football and cricket, and through the decades, he played on the village teams with his father and his grandfather, Frank. Dudley was a carpenter and ran the petrol station down at Cowbridge. His grandfather was one of the most highly-regarded builders and carpenters in Exmoor. And Frank was also the village undertaker.

Maurice has been amazed he's alive to see this small parish in the third decade of the 21st century. Timberscombe used to be populated with people like him: workers, farm labourers and those in service at big manor houses. Now it's different. Some old families remain, but there are also the newcomers – people from London, people who buy the cottages as second homes. People who have dreamed of this way of life in the English countryside, where they can be closer to themselves. As he recalls names and fits them into memories, it becomes clear that no one really ever goes away from these winding little village lanes for good. Even if they die or move, people leave behind traces of themselves. Footprints over footprints, occasions and aftermaths. Villagers or buildings or times still present, even if they aren't visible anymore.

★ ★ ★

Norman Sutton phoned me one afternoon this past winter, responding to a letter I'd written to him. He lives in Essex, and he was one of the evacuees here. I found his name through Timberscombe school records and with resources from Ancestry.com, I contacted him. I found others in the same way. Ernie Munson, who lives near Weymouth, in Dorset, and his brother John, who lives in Minehead; Eddie Gande, from West Ham, who came here with his mother and siblings and still lives in Luccombe; his sister from Barnstable, Jacqueline Gande Nunney; Charles Mehegan from Kent; James Brian Lambert from Norfolk; and Tom Robinson, from Stratford, London. They tell me about those times, what the village looked like, where they lived and with whom, how their lives changed from one day to the next. Like Maurice, they remember in bits and pieces, so many of our conversations continue for months. A sense of isolation and suffering are still with them, as though it happened yesterday and not eighty years ago.

What they remember:

Boarding trains at Paddington Station in London, crowded with other children, no one sure about where they were being taken; separating from their mothers and fathers and siblings, not knowing if they would see them again; making sure they stayed together with their brothers and sisters; how some became so homesick that they ran away and tried to get back to London.

They remember attending the funeral of the young boy from the East End, one of their own, who was run over by a lorry. Being a Boy Scout under the tutelage of a lady from the noble ranks. Practice and singing in the choir at St Petrock's. The evacuee who was a dwarf, 'a naughty little sod' who became a celebrity. The German plane that crashed in a field near the village. The Ladies - Lady Constance Ryder and Lady Audrey Anson - and the elegant Edwardian Knowle Manor where they lived. Walter Copp, always dressed in a smart, tailored suit, spent time with them and taught them about birds and insects and the names of plants and constellations - sights in the natural world a boy from the East End of London would never see. And of course there was Mrs Willis, the headmistress who kept an even temper, though she had every reason to lose it when the number of students in her classroom doubled overnight.

Eighty years ago, they left home in the morning and went to bed that night in some stranger's house on the other side of the country. Strange customs, strange accents. They were just as English as their hosts, though they might as well have been foreigners. As the months passed, they didn't know if their homes back in the city had been bombed. They didn't know if they might be orphans. Everyone had believed the war would last only a matter of months, yet it didn't end. Some children came here when they were small and stayed through puberty. After the war, some remained in Somerset. Most returned to London and other cities. When they did go back, people they once knew couldn't understand what they were saying because of their strange Somerset accents.

Whenever we talk, the evacuees wonder whatever became of each other, they wonder who is still living. Some have come back to St Petrock's Church and left notes for each other in the guest book, with the idea that somehow they might connect. A little like a note in a bottle tossed out to sea. They know it's not likely they will ever see each other again, and that they may not be alive to read each other's memories in these pages. But someone will.

Alan Hines
Timberscombe
20 July 2021

Above: Maurice Huxtable (about 1937)
(courtesy of Maurice Huxtable)

1

Leaving London

Will and Elizabeth Lambert had struggled like most young married couples do, but their future looked promising. Will's experience with machinery had secured him a good job with the contractors, Fitzgerald & Sons. In a short time, he became a plant fitter looking after all the machines, both great and small.

In late summer of 1939, at the outbreak of the Second World War, he and his neighbour in Autumn Street, Fred Gande, went to sign on for the army. They worked together at Fitzgerald & Sons, and their wives, Elizabeth and Louisa, were best friends. When the two men handed over their registration cards, Fred Gande was conscripted into the army right away, but they sent Will home. His ID card stated he was a civil engineer, a reserved occupation. He was one of those essential key workers needed to keep the home front running.

Workers in the East End lived amidst the docklands, power stations and factories like the soap works, the rubber works at Silvertown; the leather cloth works at West Ham and the chemical plant of A. Boake Roberts at Stratford. The area was densely populated. Many families lived in poverty, with a lack of decent housing. Living conditions were squalid.

Out of concern for his family's wellbeing, Will decided it would be safer if Elizabeth and their children left London. Elizabeth was reluctant to leave home, but she agreed. They figured that this part of the city, with its industrial sites, would be a prime target for German bombers.

Above: Billy Lambert (left), with his brother Brian and sister Jean and their mother, Elizabeth (1938) (courtesy of James Lambert)

Since Fred Gande would be away in the army, his wife Louisa and their three children planned to leave with the Lamberts. Elizabeth's daughter Jean was 10 and so was Maureen Gande. Billy Lambert was eight – about Eddie Gande's age – and Brian Lambert was about Patricia Gande's age.

Though he was only two, Brian Lambert believes he can recall parts of the journey today because of the way it would affect his family later. Nothing, he says, would ever be the same.

On Thursday, the 31st of August, with the situation in Europe worsening, the Minister of Health announced that the government's official evacuation of civilians from cities and other areas that were at high risk of being bombed. The government scheme, called Operation Pied Piper, made it possible to apply for evacuation aid and ensured arrangements regarding accommodation and travel. Preparations for an evacuation of this sort had been underway since the end of the Great War, when England realised that any future conflict with Germany would be by air and hand-to-hand combat.

MINISTRY OF HEALTH EVACUATION SCHEME

Above: Printed for H.M. Stationery Office by J Weiner Lt., London, W.C.1

The following day, 1½ million people were evacuated from London. They were children up to the age of 15, mothers, expectant mothers, elderly and frail people, hospital patients and the blind.

Children had to carry a kit and a Ministry of Health leaflet outlined what this should comprise: 'A handbag or case containing the child's gas mask, a change of underclothing, night clothes, house shoes or plimsolls, spare stockings or socks, a toothbrush, a comb, towel, soap and facecloth, handkerchiefs; and, if possible, a warm coat or mackintosh. Each child should bring a packet of food for the day.'

★ ★ ★

EVACUATION
OF
WOMEN AND CHILDREN
FROM LONDON. Etc.

FRIDAY, 1st SEPTEMBER.

Up and Down business trains as usual,
with few exceptions.

Main Line and Suburban services will be
curtailed while evacuation is in progress
during the day.

SATURDAY & SUNDAY,
SEPTEMBER 2nd & 3rd.

The train service will be exactly the
same as on Friday.

Remember that there will be very few
Down Mid-day business trains on Saturday.

SOUTHERN RAILWAY

Notice to Parents of Children Registered for Evacuation

READ THIS CAREFULLY — IT IS IMPORTANT.

1. The children will be taken to areas which the Government believe to be safer than the evacuating areas. Whilst no part of the country can be said to be absolutely safe, the children will have a better chance outside the towns. It is not possible to move all the children to places where they are unlikely to see anything of the war. The numbers to be moved are far too large for this, but the Government think that all the places to which children will be sent will be safer than the towns from which they will come.

2. The children will be accompanied by teachers. When they have been billeted, children will send to their parents the stamped postcard which they should take with them, giving their exact address.

3. HEALTH AND CLEANLINESS. First impressions are important, and it is essential that the people with whom our children are to be billeted should be impressed by their cleanliness. You should therefore do everything possible to ensure that your child goes away with clean clothes, clean hair and a clean body. Every Mother will wish her child to arrive at his new home in a state in which he will be welcomed.

All children will be carefully examined by the School Nurses and any instructions which are given regarding the children should be carefully carried out. If your child has sores of any kind or there is anything in connection with your child's health which you think she ought to know, don't hesitate to tell the Nurse. She is only too anxious to help you.

4. CLOTHING. The Heads of the Schools will have given you a list of clothing which it is desirable that your child should take. The following are the principal items which are given for your guidance:—

Gas Mask.
Identity Card.
Ration Book.
Food for the day.
Change of underclothing.
Night clothes.
Handkerchiefs.

Spare stockings or socks.
House shoes or plimsolls.
Warm coat or mackintosh.
Toothbrush.
Comb.
Towel.

The child should wear the overcoat or mackintosh and his thickest boots or shoes, and should be warmly clothed.

The luggage must not be more than the child can carry. Other clothes needed can be sent on later.

You will be responsible for renewing the child's clothing while away.
Gas masks should be slung over the shoulder and not carried in the luggage.

5. FOOD. As it may take some hours to reach the destination, every child must be given sufficient food for the day. The following items would make a good meal:—
Sandwiches (egg or cheese).
Packets of nuts or seedless raisins.
Dry biscuits (with little packets of cheese).

Barley sugar (rather than chocolate).
Apple, orange.
Liquids should not be carried by children.

6. LUGGAGE. The most suitable luggage carrier both for the journey and for use away is the rucksack. This is strapped on the back and leaves the arms free. If a rucksack is too expensive a haversack would be cheaper and is a good substitute.

All property belonging to a child should be marked with the child's name.
If you have not a haversack or small suitcase for your child, a pillow case makes a better carrier than a parcel. Do not load up your child with parcels.

7. LABELS. Two labels will be supplied by the school for your child. One should be affixed to his luggage, and the other, in the case of a girl, tied round her neck; and for a boy, fixed to the lapel of his jacket.

8. RATION BOOKS. Be sure that your child has his ration book with him. If pages of coupons out of his book have been deposited with retailers, ask for their return and put the pages in the ration book.

Both the ration book and the identity card should be securely packed in the child's luggage and not given him to hold.

9. MEDICAL AND DENTAL TREATMENT. Unless I hear from you to the contrary it will be assumed that you give your consent to a doctor's or dentist's advice being carried out when your child is away from home.

10. It is realised that you will be anxious about your child, but I can assure you that as far as it is in the power of the Teachers, every care will be taken to look after him or her.

H. BOYES WATSON,
Chief Education Officer.

Across the country that morning, on the Dunster Castle polo field
in Exmoor, Somerset, the 101st Dunster Show was just getting
underway. This agricultural show was the district's biggest event of
the summer, with a food hall, trade stands and exhibitions and quality
entertainment for all, including ferret racing. Divisions for horses,
cattle and sheep attracted competitors from all over the county. When
word came that Germany had attacked Poland, all competition and
judging stopped. The band ceased playing.

After months of planning, reception parties in Williton and Minehead felt prepared for the evacuees. It was as though they were going
into battle themselves. First, the formation of reception committees.
Then surveys of every village and hamlet, house-to-house visits, school
visits, enlisting billeting officers, recruitment of dozens of volunteers,
especially women. Billets had to be made ready.

Evacuees only had a few hours warning in the early dawn hours
when they were told: 'This is it! We're going.' They were leaving their

mums and dads, their homes, gathering in the school yard, just as they had practiced for the past year. Then Paddington Station. A commotion of children they knew from school and children they didn't recognise from other schools, mothers, teachers crowded in railway cars. None knew their destination.

In her book, *Exmoor Village, Celebrating the Enduring Landscape of Exmoor and its people over 50 years,* Hilary Binding wrote that Roy Clenappa helped co-ordinate the evacuees journey. He remembered: "Nobody knew where their destination would be, though I had an idea it would be the Oxford area. As children were stomping across the platform, a porter called out: "*Mine* your feet! *Mind* your *heads*! *Watch it!*' Minehead. Watchet. I whispered to my wife: "That's where they're going".'

Eighty years later, the evacuees from Timberscombe remembered that morning.

Thomas Robinson

Tommy Robinson was nine years old on that day.

'*My father had been wounded at the Battle of The Somme, where his brother was killed. He knew London would suffer dearly.*

'*Many of us children lined up outside Gainsborough Road School in West Ham, London E.15, by West Ham Station. Mothers and relations across the road gathered to see us off. My mother was in tears, as were many others… There were five Robinson children in the queue, three brothers, a sister and myself, Tom, aged nine. Ernie was 13, Joyce 11, Bill was seven, and Jim was five. My sister Joyce and I worried that our younger brothers and sisters might be separated.*

'*We all had our gas masks on our shoulders as we boarded the train, especially laid on for evacuees.*'

Ernie Munson

George Munson and his wife Dora, who were both 39 years old, lived in Plaistow. He was a carpenter and a joiner, though unable to work or enlist because he had fallen off scaffolding and damaged his spine.

They had six children and wanted to get their younger children out of London before they left themselves.

Ernie Munson has memories of West Ham then, when he was seven years old: lorries delivering groceries, trams, buses. Horse and carts delivering coal. He remembers the park where they would play with other children from the neighbourhood, including Eddie Gande. The air was yellow, thick with smog, and putrid smelling from industry around the dock works.

Ernie remembers the morning he and his sisters, Iris and Grace, and his brother Sid gathered at the Manor Road School.

'Waking up in my own home, in the bosom of my family, going to school with cases and gas masks. I had a tag on my lapel, with my name, age, and religion.'

Ernie remembers mums and dads on pavements, waving as they walked past, and then boarding the train. Hours later, when it was pitch dark, they would be miles away from home, in a little village called Timberscombe.

Roy Smith

Five out of seven Smith children were evacuated from West Ham to Timberscombe: three boys and two girls. Harry, Royston, Raymond, Mary and Iris. Their two older sisters, Helen and Elsie, already had jobs and stayed in London.

Roy was seven and already a con artist. He knew how to size up any situation and work it to his advantage. He commanded attention from his siblings, in fact, from everyone he came into contact with, because of his wits – but to a great extent, because he was a dwarf. Later in life, being 50 inches tall and muscle-bound brought him notoriety among stage and film celebrities and London underworld types.

'Being little, I had a chip on my shoulder when I went to the Gainsborough Road School in West Ham.'

He always saw himself as a social outcast, although family and acquaintances said that this was through his own choosing. He claimed to have come from a gypsy family, to be Romany with mixed Jewish blood, like the infamous Kray brothers.

Toward the end of Roy's life, the author, George Tremlett recorded Roy's memories in his book, *Little Legs: Muscleman of Soho*.

'*Our home at Wallace Road was in West Ham, right on top of the London docks. We parked our caravan and trailer out in the yard.*

'*My father was a street bookmaker, but he could turn his hand at anything, like me. The East End was different in those days, just before the war. There weren't so many motor cars. The muffin men used to walk with a tray of muffins on their head, ringing a handbell. "Muffins, your muffins, muffins I got!" At weekends, a woman came round with a donkey cart, brought rock cockles, mussels, whelks, shrimps and crayfish.*'

Roy tells entertaining stories about his time as an evacuee in Timberscombe, though his version of the chronology and the events themselves are sometimes distorted. As he relates it:

'*We were bombed four times during the war. The first bomb fell a short time after the war started. It wasn't long before us kids were evacuated.*

'*The first bomb wasn't a direct hit. It fell on the Jewish cemetery across the road. We should have been all right because we had an Anderson at the bottom of our garden.*

Anderson shelters were constructed from corrugated iron sheets bolted together at the top, with steel plates at either end. They were half buried in the ground with earth heaped on top to protect them from bomb blasts.

'*After the air raid warning, we all went down there, but my mum came back to the house to make a cup of tea, and the blast blew out all the windows and the kitchen sink clean off the wall. The sink was stone, and it fell across her legs, trapping her to the floor.*

'*After that, Mum spent a long time in and out of hospital, because the weight of the sink and the force of the blast had broken her femur.*'

Roy wrote that his mother's accident led to her children's evacuation.

'*I cried because I had never been away from home before. My sisters, Mary and Iris, came with me, and so did my brothers, Harry and Raymond. We were to report at the Gainsborough Road School, where the teachers gave us all a gas mask in a cardboard box to sling across our shoulders, and a little bag of sandwiches and orange juice to keep us going on the journey.'*

★ ★ ★

Many parents decided they would make their own arrangements for their children and themselves. While figures show that one and a half million took advantage of the government scheme, two million made their own independent arrangements. Posters were plastered all over the city, advising, 'Mothers, send them out of London', with a picture of anxious children looking up at their mums with alarm. Railway stations were overrun and additional trains had to be scheduled to move the crowds of children out of London.

Charles 'Chas' Mehegan

In 1944, when Charles Mehegan was eleven, he and his seven-year-old brother James came to Timberscombe, not as official evacuees, but via arrangement by their mother and father.

'The Germans were launching V1 rockets (doodlebugs) on London in Woolwich, close to Woolwich Arsenal. One blew the roof off our house, which prompted my father to send my brother James and I to live with my aunt Rosie in Timberscombe. All I remember of the journey was being on the train with my mother and a soldier giving her his seat.'

2

Timberscombe 1939

The medieval village of Dunster lies on the Bristol Channel coast. It grew up around Dunster Castle, which was built on the Tor by William de Moyon shortly after the Norman Conquest of 1066. Several Iron Age hillforts in the vicinity give evidence that the area had been occupied for thousands of years. The Luttrell family, who were lords of the manor beginning in the 14th century, remodelled the castle and by the 20th century it had become a stately Victorian home. Nestled below the castle are winding cobblestone streets, thatched cottages, the Priory Church of St. George, a dove cote, and a tithe barn. In the mid 17th century, George Luttrell built a Yarn Market and the village became a centre for wool and cloth production.

Three miles inland from Dunster, past the hamlet of Cowbridge, the road curves left around a steep bank and Timberscombe appears. Except for the late 20th-century addition of some bungalows, the architectural bones of the Somerset village appear much as they did more than a century ago. Houses and cottages are red stone or rendered, a few roofs still thatched. Other dwellings fill in what would have been blank spaces on earlier ordinance maps. From this approach, the tower of St Petrock's Church appears to be at the centre of the village.

Come around that bend and an Edwardian-style house called Sunnyside is on the right. In 1939, a gardener named Tom Brewer and his wife, Maud, lived here with their three grown children. They took in two young evacuee sisters from London. In those days,

Sunnyside was also the local GP surgery two mornings a week: Dr Meade-King on Tuesday at 11:30, and Dr Valentine and Dr Forester every Thursday at 11:00.

The brook that meanders through the village runs into the River Avill. Its sound is constant. On this morning, in the present, there's birdsong you never hear in the city. Occasionally, the clank of hammering somewhere or the clatter of a tractor or other large agricultural machines driven by a farm worker may barrel through the twisting narrow street. Almost at once, it's quiet again, except for the brook. Sounding just as gentle as it did the first weekend in September 1939, when the population of school children in Timberscombe doubled from 35 to 70.

At the center of the village, just past The Lion Inn, stone steps lead up to the churchyard and St Petrock's. The 15th century Anglican church is built of stone and comprises a chancel, a rare wooden rood screen and loft. There's a Jacobian pulpit, restored wall paintings and a piscina dating from the 1400s. Richard Ellsworth, Esq. rebuilt the tower in 1708. It contains a clock and a peal of eight bells. The churchyard cross dates from the 1300s and the yew tree is over 440 years old.

This past year, workers unblocked the south door that had been sealed since the Reformation. Excavation of the hillside revealed evidence of an earlier settlement, burial remains from the 8th century, remnants of coffin handles, nails and hardware and human bones. Radiocarbon dating set the finds back to the year 777. This evidence shows that the location where St Petrock's stands had been a place of worship in a Saxon settlement, long before the current church was built in the 15th century.

Many tombstones in the church yard have fallen and now line the stone wall along the perimeter. Weather has chipped at names and dates and to read inscriptions takes a practiced eye.

Down a walkway that winds through tombstones near the yew tree at the north door, there's a wrought-iron archway and gate with an

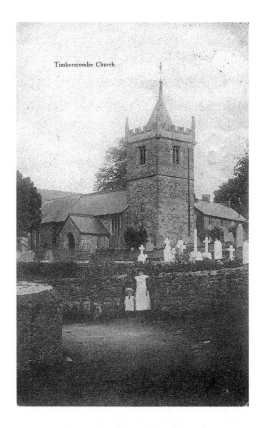

Timberscombe Church.

Above: St. Petrock's Church

electric lantern on its apex. Deep cobblestone steps descend to street level. A late 19th century stone drinking trough, rectangular and set on four stone blocks and a plinth, is at the bottom of the church steps. It has a gabled top with a pair of trefoil headed niches, masked above.

This morning, children head for the Timberscombe First School at the other end of the village, just as they did in 1939 when Katherine Willis was the school mistress. Mrs Willis lived at School House Cottage next to the school with her husband Bill and their four-year-old son Michael.

When the war began, The Reading Room was still standing on the Glebe, down at the bottom of the churchyard and across from the vicarage. It was constructed of corrugated iron on a stone foundation in 1913. Any man over 16 living in Timberscombe could become a member by paying a subscription. Members could play cards and draughts, but gambling was forbidden. Books belonging to the room could be read on the premises and only taken away by special permission. Anyone swearing or using foul language would be fined 6d.

Back at the Old Dunster Road – before the county put in the bypass – the narrow road curves around a terrace of red-stone buildings. It winds past Game House, at one time a pub called the Rose and Crown. Burrow Cottage, the cottage at the end of the terrace, was known as Berrowcote in 1939. It was the post office as early as 1841.

Eva Jane Floyde lived in the cottage behind it. She was the Post Office Deliverer and in summers, sold homemade ice cream on the corner.

Next to Eva Jane Floyde's cottage was Frank Huxtable's garage/ workshop and Pump Cottage, where he lived with his wife Eva. Maurice Huxtable's grandfather, Frank, a wheelwright as well as a carpenter, employed local men on building projects around the village, including holiday houses at Dunster Beach. Eva Huxtable was proprietress of the Motor Spirit Service Station in front of their cottage.

In 1939, Timberscombe had four grocery shops – Loveridge's on Church Street; Jeffrey's and Coles on Jubilee Terrace; and The Stores on Brook Street, next to the butcher shop. In later years, the butcher shop became Ye Olde Malt House, Maurice Huxtable's future residence. Coles Saddlery was across from the butcher shop. Sam Heard, who owned the pub, the Lion Hotel, operated the motor omnibus and was also the newsagent. He lived at the hotel with his wife, Gertrude.

On the far side of the village, a dusty sloping lane leads up to Croydon House Farm. Through a gate on the left, a path zigzags up the hill. Once reaching the top, it opens up to sky and the vast Timberscombe Commons. A 360 degree view above hedgerows and gardens, sheep, church bells, above green rolling hills, a patchwork of tilled fields, the village of Wootton Courtney sheltered in the distance between a valley and Dunkery Beacon, the highest point on Exmoor

Above: Reading Room and Rectory

Above: Jeffrey's on Jubilee Terrace

Above: Delbridge, one of the shops on Jubilee Terrace

Above: The south end of Brook Street

and in Somerset. Dunster Forest, to the north, is part of the 'Royal Forest of Exmoor', established by Henry II. Trails in the forest were trod two centuries ago by the poets William Wordsworth and Samuel Coleridge when they lived nearby.

Down in the village once more, pass the Methodist chapel headed up Church Street and before you reach Beasley Farm is an Iron Age Hillfort, "officially" discovered in 1992. For decades, fragments of iron slag have been found here, a type identified with smithing, suggesting an iron works was within the enclosure at some point.

The Cowbridge sawmill is at the other end of the village. Maurice Huxtable remembers how blacksmith, Sam Grabham, 'shoeing horses, would cuss and carry on, him and his son Ken, cutting wood up at the mill'.

The entry and drive that winds around to Knowle Manor is further on, headed back toward Dunster. It's a fine mansion in well-wooded grounds of about 50 acres, a private home today as well as a venue for weddings and parties. During the war, it was the residence of Lady Constance Ryder and her sister, Lady Audrey Anson.

On the first weekend of September 1939, villagers were prepared to take in an unknown number of displaced children and mothers from London, a cosmopolitan world unlike few locals could imagine.

Two days before the evacuees arrived, the school managers met to discuss the question of blackout curtains and suitable heated locations for evacuees to meet for afternoon classes. They decided the vicar, Rev. Isidore Lach-Szyrma, should write to the Education Authorities in Taunton to ask for direction. They also wanted to know whether the county would bear the cost, as it did not concern the Timberscombe children.

A month later, the reply came that the County Education Committee could not cover the cost of blackout material for the school – or heating of any recreational buildings for the evacuee children. Mrs Willis and the teachers coming in from London would just have to make do.

3

Arrival

Teachers in large cities across the country had been evacuated, along with their pupils. Questions were fired at them from every direction – not only from children, but from anxious parents too. Before the groups could proceed from the school grounds to the station, teachers had to make sure every child was present with proper name tags and luggage.

One teacher was assigned to each carriage, though sometimes carriages shared by different schools were assigned two or three teachers. Queues formed at the toilets. Some children were too nervous to wait their turn and the teacher in charge had to find clean underwear and tidy up the child.

Operation Pied Piper required so many additional trains that normal timetables for express and non-stop runs were abandoned. Trips were slow, and sometimes trains came to a halt outside a junction for a half hour.

Brian Lambert
Brian remembers many soldiers on the train, which meant that his family and the Gandes had to sit in the corridor on suitcases.
   'My mother told me that when we arrived, no one knew where we were.'

Jacqueline Gande Nunney
Jackie Nunney, Louisa Gande's daughter, was born in Minehead several years after her mother arrived in Timberscombe. Her mother

Above: Newly arrived evacuees (September 1939)
(courtesy of Minehead Museum)

told her she and Jackie's brother and sisters left Paddington Station in London for Taunton, then changed trains for Minehead. Louisa said no one could see any landmarks in the passing countryside because the train windows had been blacked out.

'In Minehead, one woman got off of the train, saw the sea front, and said: "I think we're in Somerset".'

Though the Gandes had Elizabeth Lambert and her children as travelling companions, Jackie says her mother was still a single mother with three children under five. The responsibilities and loneliness were a struggle for her.

'In time, all niceties and graces just wore away because she had a lot to cope with. Mum had been one of nine children, and not a cuddly type. We got that from Dad.'

Later that first day, evacuees spilled out of trains at the Minehead railway station and were met by the reception committee and billeting officers. Evacuees who were to be billeted in Minehead were separated from those that would be housed elsewhere.

Besides local councils, teachers and railway staff, Operation Pied Piper authorities had turned to the Women's Voluntary Service across the country as Britain prepared for war. Over a million women volunteered. They were known as "women in green". Upon their arrival, evacuees were steered up the Avenue by Minehead WVS volunteers to the Regal Ballroom, where they were herded aboard buses.

Thomas Robinson

'Those of us left were on our byway coach to Timberscombe, a village about five miles from Minehead.'

Once they arrived in Timberscombe, Tommy remembers being at the school as potential hosts gathered around, inspecting them, looking for the most presentable specimens. The new arrivals were drinking chocolate and having biscuits. They were tired, hungry, many of them in soiled pants. Humiliated at waiting to be picked. Children and adults alike looked frightened and were tearful. They were far from home and uncertain how much longer this ordeal would continue.

'We arrived and were escorted to the school where some of the local parents were picking which children they wanted, sometimes breaking up young brothers and sisters. My elder brother Ernie and sister Joyce were arguing who would take the younger ones with them if we were split up.'

Locals gave the names on the children's tags to the billeting officers standing by with clipboards. The billeting officers had to collect registration slips signed by each of the parents if the children were going to get cash for food and lodging from the government. They were paid by taking a form to the local post office. Most hosts were eager to give the children a new home for as long as it was necessary. Older boys of about 12 went quickly – perhaps to help with farm work. No one wanted to host the teachers.

'*Women chose girls, someone to help with the washing up, cleaning up, laundry. Older girls especially. We had five of us in our family. No one wanted us.*'

It took some hours before the children were matched with hosts, and those that felt they were going to get left behind were in tears.

'*In the end, there were about 16 of us left in the hall who hadn't been chosen. Then a lady walked in, she seemed to take charge, and we walked out to the street, where we got into two cars. One was a big Buick with a chauffeur and another a Morris eight.*'

Ernie Munson

'*We got off the coach and saw three long medieval vestry windows and thought it was a church but it was the school.*'

Ernie remembers being in the Timberscombe school, after having arrived from Minehead. All the activity was confusing, and he was just trying to stay close to his younger brother, Sid, and sisters, Iris and Grace.

Above: Grace, Iris, Ernie, and Sid (about 1938)
(courtesy of Ernie Munson)

John Gratton, his mother Phyllis, and Joyce Thurtle,
the evacuee who lived with them (1944) (courtesy of John Gratton)

John Gratton

'At the end of '43 we had an evacuee come live with us. I remember there was a load of kids, evacuees, came up our street in Dunster Marsh at night, surrounding a big hand cart loaded up with suitcases and corn flake boxes some had used to pack their belongings, all tied up with binder cord. And pushing the handcart was the local vicar and there were a couple of ladies with him, distributing the children.

'The vicar stopped outside our house, and my mother went out to see him. "I've got a girl called Joycie Thurtle," he said. "She's about 12." And because my mum was very young, only 20-odd, he says, "You're much more her age, rather than put her with older people." And he said: "Would you take her in as an evacuee?" So this girl came and lived with us. It was a great help to my mother because she was on her own.'

* * *

Evacuees living with strangers were eligible to receive billeting allowances from the government evacuation scheme, while those living in homes, either through family or personal connections, were not. Two 'unofficial evacuees' were Patricia Robinson and her sister, Jeanne.

Patricia Robinson

Patricia and Jeanne Robinson were evacuated to Kiln House to live with Harry and Annie Prole, their maternal grandparents. They had visited since they were very young, so they were familiar with their grandparents' house and the village, and a quite a lot of family lived in the village and the area.

In her memoir, *Away and Home – World War II*, Pat Robinson Herniman writes: "Jeanne, aged 10, knew why we were going, but I was not quite eight and very inquisitive. They spared me the upset of knowing the reason for the visit.

"Gran and Grandad welcomed their "little maids" and we were happy to see them, but this time I was anxious when Mum and Dad set off for home without us. At Kiln House, we were lucky to be with family, but it was much more of a challenge for the official evacuees, with three million children being sent to complete strangers in various parts of Britain in Operation Pied Piper. The Daily Herald newspaper dated 4 September 1939 recorded that by 2 September, 485,900 had already reached their destinations."

Later, on the night of their arrival in Timberscombe, two young East End boys followed along after the couple they would live with. As they made their way in the dark up Duck Street, one boy leaned toward his brother: 'Innit funny? Buildings standing on their own and not all connected?'

4

Billeting

Winston Churchill's Home Secretary, Sir John Anderson, was put in charge of the Operation Pied Piper scheme. He decided that if someone lived in a reception area, they would be required to take evacuees into their homes. If they refused, and didn't have a good reason for not doing so, they could be taken to court and fined.

A billeter received 10s. 6d. from the government for taking in a child, and if they took in more than one, they would get another 8s. 6d. per head. All evacuees had to hand over rationing books to their hosts.

Mothers who went with their children under the scheme were lodged in billets. The government paid the householder 5s. a week for the mother, and 3s. a week for each child. This meant the mother had to buy and arrange the preparing of her own food, and this usually caused tension between the billeter and evacuee.

Thomas Robinson
'We arrived along the Dunster Road to a lodge with big iron gates and drove up to a great big mansion house surrounded by a circular lawn and other scenery. As we reached the front door, it was opened by a man in a black suit and bow tie, the butler. Beside him was a woman in whites – "the cook".

'We were given a cup of hot milk which we couldn't drink; it was too rich. The milk was from their herd of pedigree Jersey cows, which had won ribbons at cattle shows. The Ladies had placed the ribbons on the cowshed walls. Then we went to bed.

'Our rooms were all at the rear of the house. The boys' room had about eight or nine beds, camp beds, which occupied about 30% of this enormous room. The girl's rooms were smaller, about six girls sharing two rooms.

'Knowle consisted of many fields, woods, gardens and animal enclosures, the farmyard, cowsheds, pigsty and aviary. The stable was a large rotunda building, with a house to the left and another to the right of entrance. In the stables were two large cart horses for ploughing and other work, Colonel and Pleasant, male and female, a large pedigree bull, and various other animals and young cattle.

'The servants at the house were at first, the butler, the cook, the maids, ladies maid, and four others, plus a butler's boy and our carer. On the farm was the bailiff, the horseman who was also the chauffeur, and the handyman, who was the back lodge keeper. The main lodge keeper was the gardener and his son, and farm hands from the village.

'There was an orchard with various apple trees – Worcester's, Orange Pippins, Cox's and others - including cider apples for the workers, which were fermented in a well in the barn for haymakers and harvesters. Fruit and vegetables were grown in a large walled garden.

'The two ladies who lived at Knowle Manor were Lady Constance Ryder and Lady Audrey Anson. Everyone in the house and in Timberscombe spoke to them as 'My Lady', as we did, and raised their hats. They ran the village.'

★ ★ ★

The Lamberts and the Gandes were also billeted at Knowle, at the farm at the back of the property instead of the manor house. They were given the two living areas in the stable block where farm labourers sometimes lived. In front was a quadrangle with a stone arching entrance where the bull and cattle were kept. Elizabeth and her children stayed in the accommodations to the left; and the Gandes stayed on the opposite side.

Louisa Gande and her children lived here for a brief period before moving to The Bungalow on the lane behind Knowle farm. Their cousin, six-year-old Bernard Gande, was with them for a short time before he was billeted with Mrs Webber at The Gardens.

Ernie Munson's parents, George and Dora Munson, arrived in Timberscombe a short time later, and they moved into the Gande's previous quarters in the stables.

Brian Lambert

'It was a cold place with slab floors. The reception area had a stone trough and a boiler in one corner. My mother boiled the water, put it in the trough and we would have a bath or do our washing. They mixed animal feed in the trough, too. Then in back was a tack room. This was all on the ground floor. We slept in the bedroom, which was one flight of stairs up in the loft area.

'Lady Constance and Lady Audrey picked Mother to work in the kitchen in the main house. Mrs Gande helped with other chores and in the fields.

'A large group of children were staying in the main house. I believe they were orphans.'

Jacqueline Gande Nunney

Not long after Jackie's mother moved to The Bungalow, her father had a weekend leave from the Army Engineers. Jackie was conceived on Fred Gande's weekend visit and then born at Irnham Lodge in Minehead.

Later, the "women in green" moved Louisa and her children once again, from The Bungalow at Knowle to Croydon Farm. John Thackrah, a herdsman, and his wife Margaret, also lived at Croydon with their young daughters, Margaret Elizabeth and Barbara, who were Eddie and Patricia Gande's age.

'Croydon Farm was a big manor house up past The Great House, past Holes Square, and through the woods. It was all orchards – plums, apples, pears. All the men were off to war and so the place wasn't well-cared-for. Coming from London, Mum wasn't a gardener.'

Louisa and her four children left Croydon Farm because new evacuees, the three Tredego children, the three Perfect children, the three Gilbert children and Peter Gilmore – all from the Manor Road

School in Erith, Kent – moved in. The Gande family was re-billeted once again, this time to Luccombe.

Eddie Gande

The Gandes were re-billeted four times. In each new home, Eddie remembers how his mother took on any task that came up to maintain the house and provide a home for her children.

'She could repair boots, make clothes. She repaired things in the village. At Croydon, we had the place to ourselves. We had rooms downstairs and the use of the kitchen. She went about dusting rooms through the house and kept things tidy. We weren't supposed to go into other rooms, but she showed us the shiny table in the dining room.

'There was a massive walled garden with an outside privy. It had 'four holes for four bums.'

Ernie Munson

The four Munson children were separated the night they arrived. Splitting up siblings happened several times in Timberscombe. Norman Sutton was separated from his brothers. Evelyn and Margaret Talbot went to Sunnyside with Tom and Maud Brewer, while their older sister Eunice was billeted with Mrs Coles at Coombe House.

Ernie, seven, and Sid Munson, five, were billeted with an older couple who resided at Hillview, Thomas and Frances Veale. Tom was 75 and Frances was 53. The boys had their own bedroom that looked out over the garden. From the beginning, Ernie says, there were strains and complications. The couple didn't know how, or weren't inclined, to give two little boys a home. Often, they were left on their own. Both missed their parents and home in London. Like a lot of other children that day, they had been swept away so fast that they hadn't realised what it all meant. Sid became distraught, and the Veales contacted the billeting officers to take the boys off their hands.

'WVS ladies put children with different people if others didn't get on with it.'

Sid was taken to the hostel in Taunton where other evacuee children were gathered who experienced the same kinds of emotional traumas, being separated from family and home. Ernie moved to Ernest and Rosina Clatworthy's house on Duck Street, today called Great House Road. When Sid returned, Lady Ryder asked that the boys be re-billeted to the main house at Knowle Manor.

Their sisters, Grace, 10, and Iris, 12, were billeted with Henry and Edith Baker on Church Street. Not long after their arrival, the girls returned to London. Other children and mothers with children were doing the same. When bombing began in the early spring, Grace and Iris came back to Timberscombe and lived with Mrs Ray at The Old Mill. Eventually, they were also given a room in the main house at Knowle Manor. When their parents, George and Dora, arrived, the family took over the Gandes' quarters in the stables.

Ernest Clatworthy was a farm carter and 51 years old. Rosina was 10 years older. When he lived at the Clatworthy's, Ernie saw his sisters and others from West Ham at school every day. Other than that, he was alone most of the time, except for the Clatworthy's 27-year-old son, Bill.

'Bill worked as a quarryman. He was over six feet, a 'gentle giant'. He was a lovely big fellow. Never made a fuss. Gave me two shillings every weekend out of his wages. And a pocketknife. Wouldn't say boo to a ghost. One time, he went up on Croydon Hill, rabbiting. A ferret got stuck, and Bill waited all night long for the ferret to come back. The next morning, he got up and went to work. People in the village had nicknamed him 'Lightning' because he was slow.

'Stairs went up from the front door at the Clatworthy's. The landing at the top of the stairs was wide enough for a single bed. That's where I slept. I had a curtain around my bed. Bill's room faced the street.

'A picture of the Clatworthy's cottage is still sharp in my mind to this day. And also an image of Eva Jane Floyde, going past the Richards' and the Clatworthy's on Duck Street, delivering the mail.'

* * *

Most households in the village were small cottages, not on the grand scale of houses like Knowle, Bickham or Croydon. Making room for more people was a challenge. Rooms had to be re-arranged. New beds had to be found.

At first sight, some villagers assumed the children they had agreed to take into their homes had fleas. And some did, and impetigo and scabies, too. This was the case in reception areas all over England. Some, host parents discovered, lacked proper toilet training, or didn't know the proper way to use a knife and fork, or failed to give basic hygiene a thought. Others had never slept in a bed. On the first night of the evacuees arrival, one billeter thought the child in her care had run away, but then she found him asleep under the bed, "where I always sleep," he told her.

In the early months of the war, goodwill in reception areas deteriorated for several reasons – the condition in which many of the evacuees arrived, the absence of expected air attacks on London, and a belief that some parents back in London were better off and were saving money at the expense of people in the reception areas. Throughout the winter of 1939–40, complaints among villagers continued. Taking care of a child often cost more than hosts expected. Laundry, clothing and other incidentals added up to more than just room and board.

Nearly all evacuee mothers were dependent on their husbands for financial support. In most cases, husbands could send funds to keep their wives and children, since basic accommodation was provided for them by the government. Inevitably, the cost of maintaining two separate households on a husband's low wages became too much of a burden.

As far as many hosts were concerned, the government's allocation of 5s. a week for the mother and 3s. for the child covered basic bedroom accommodation. For the mother and her children, it was like being cooped up in part of a house. Having her children underfoot made it difficult to carry out chores, such as the washing and ironing, having a bath, or providing cooked meals. Most times, they were expected to perform these tasks in their bedroom.

Norman Sutton

Norman Sutton, from Canning Town, was one of 10 children. He and three of his brothers were evacuees.

'No one wanted four boys from one family, so Peter, the oldest, and Adrian, the youngest, seven, went with the Bryans in Brook House. Peter was almost 14, the age when he would leave school. I was nine and billeted with the Slades, and Jack, 12, lived with the Ferrises at Cendle Terrace. George Ferris was a farm carter. He and his wife Alice had four children – three daughters and a son.

'In the beginning, there was more switching around. Evacuees moved from one household to another. Jack was a bit of a rebel, always looking for mischief. Maybe the Ferrises thought he was a bad influence on their son John, who was about the same age. Soon Jack left the Ferris's to stay with the Bakers in Brook Street.'

The Slades house, where Norman was billeted, was called Holes Square. Down the slope of road in front of it was an orchard and past it, a field of willows. The Slades had one daughter in the land army and another living in Porlock. Their oldest son was away in the army. At home was a 14-year-old son who was too old to be friends with Norman, and two daughters. Norman had his own room.

The Hollands, who lived next door in Hill Cottage, were gypsies. Trinet Holland, her father John and brother John Jr. and her Uncle Henry. Trinet ran the family business, which was listed in the 1939 Register as 'waste materials'. They collected and sold clothes, mushrooms and rabbits. They were one of the few families in the village who owned a car.

New houses were built later at the bottom of the hill where there had been an orchard. The lane was called Willow Bank.

Norman remembers the pack horse bridge next to The Old Mill. A cockerel from the Old Mill claimed the territory as his. He would position himself near the bridge and not let the children cross on their way to school. If they tried, he would attack them.

'An old lady sat at the front window in a flat at the top of the steps and watched me every time I went out. Then she'd report whatever she saw me doing to the Slades. Climbing trees, throwing rocks at the cockerel, which I had to do so we could pass and get to school. And a time or two, she told them she saw me smoking.'

Oil lamps and candles were used in the house, he remembers. There was running water, but the privy was outside. Since there was no electricity, the Slades used accumulators, which were energy storing devices. They had to be lugged down the hill, past the Old Mill and down Church Street to Loveridge's whenever they needed to be recharged. Usually, the task was left to Norman.

'Jimmy Jeffrey had a shop across from the Lion Inn, and he was also a tailor. He had a greenhouse up near the quarry, just above Holes Square, where he grew vegetables for his store.'

Roy Smith

'We were taken to this massive mansion called Knowle, where Lady Constance Ryder and her sister Lady Audrey Anson looked after us like VIPs. We had never seen anything like it, and for us East End kids, the next three or four years were the finest years of our lives.

'Eighteen of us were taken into their home, which was the most luxurious place we had ever seen. Three drives led away from the mansion across the park, one leading to the road to Timberscombe, the second to Minehead, and the third to Wootton Courtenay. They also owned two farms and part of the river, which used to get flooded.

'That was where I learned to love the trout; they came in swarms, similar to salmon, and you knew which way they were going, so all you had to do was sit there taking it easy, having a rest, and then you'd fish them out with a net. Nice fish, about a pound and a half.

'In the park they had ponies and so I could ride bareback in the local gymkhanas. The sisters had separate herds of Jerseys and Guernseys, and

they let me have a jersey cow of my own as a pet. She was blind, and we called her Bumbles. I used to take her around the fields on a halter. Now, a cow's tongue is rougher than a horse's and she used to lick me because she liked me; she always knew when I was there from my voice, and I was the one who was allowed to lead her in for milking. They didn't have milking machines down there in those days. I used to milk her myself.

'Lady Constance was a wonderful, motherly sort of woman, really, although she had never had children of her own. She worried about me because I was little, and gave me a room of my own with a beautiful Chesterfield settee instead of a bed.

'An old battle-axe of a cook, Ma Chaplin, cooked for us and for them, and she used to say, "Royston, Royston, you're a naughty little elf" because I was a right little sod all the time I was there, playing tricks, and going out across the fields, poaching rabbits, which I would leave on her kitchen shelf.

'They had three gamekeepers, but the main one was a boy called Bolsie, who had a 12-bore shotgun. He would never miss a bleeding rabbit, and used to take me out with him, shooting rooks through their nests. It's unfortunate, but rooks are pests and they've got to go. I learned a hell of a lot in Somerset. I used to go picking whortleberries, which are like a blackcurrant, and it was good poaching country.

'Bolsie taught me such a lot. He was a shotgun merchant, and I said to him one day, "Can I go out with yer?" He used to walk around the fields with his gun under his arm and a bag like a moneybag around his waist in which he kept two ferrets. He would stick them down a hole with no nets and stand there waiting with his 12-bore. Then when the rabbits would pop out, BANG! Then he says, "I'll teach you how to do the snares." And he taught me to find their runs, the best places to put a snare, and how to set the pegs.

'The rabbits were heavy for me because of my legs. One day, I was out on my own, using fishing nets over the holes because I didn't have a gun. You could hear the rabbits coming. You sit on the ground and hear the pads of their feet as they run through the burrows, so you know when one is coming out. I heard this one running and went to grab him in the net, but he came through so fast that he knocked me over on my back.

'Normally, you grab a rabbit by the back legs, put two fingers of your other hand behind his neck and pull – quick. That kills them. But I have short arms and when I got this one in the net, he fought me before I could grab his legs; then he clawed me to pieces and got away – so I gave the ferret a slap!'

Ernie Munson

'Mr Bowles was the chauffeur. No one would ever dare call him Bolsie.'

John Gratton

'Joycie Thurtle was like my older sister. I was about four. She was used to younger brothers and sisters because she came from a family of 13 in the middle of London. My mother was issued an evacuee passbook, which allowed her to have 10 shillings a week off the state for her care.

'Joyce took a milk route up at Dunster Castle. The dairy was halfway up castle hill. And she had a hand cart with little milk churns and ladles in it and some milk in bottles. And she went around Dunster, dishing out milk in jugs. I used to go with her on a Saturday morning.

'Food was scarce. One of my grandfathers had this amazing dog called June that we used to take up into the deer park, under the noses of the Luttrells, and hunt rabbits. We lived on rabbits for about four years. This dog used to catch seven or eight rabbits on an outing. My grandfather used to bring them home and skin them. He sold the skins to a person called Gypsy Holland. John and Trinet Holland who lived in Timberscombe up at Holes Square. They used to come through on a pony and cart every Monday morning and collect these rabbit skins. I was only about four or five, and I used to have to stand in the road with these rabbit skins and the Hollands would pay me a thruppence for a rabbit skin.'

Chas Mehegan

'My aunt and uncle had two boys much the same age as us – Sidney, the eldest, and Edward. Aunt Rosie was a big, intimidating woman who looked like my mother, but was nothing like her otherwise. Today, most children

Above: Chas Mehegan – age 7 (courtesy of Charles Mehegan)

know their relatives, but in those days, aunts and uncles were remote. You didn't really know them.

'The house was the last one in a row of terrace houses. A long garden led down to where a wide stream ran. Maurice Huxtable lived two houses down. My uncle, Ivan Bircham, was a mail deliverer. His long postal round took him most of the day as he cycled many miles to outlying houses and farms. Sometimes he would bring back rabbits he was given, and I would watch as he sat on a large flat stone by the stream at the bottom of the garden gutting them.

'One day, my aunt said, "A parcel has come from your mother." When she opened it, there were two pairs of new boots. She said, "Isn't that nice? Your mother has sent my two boys some new boots." The next morning we were given her two sons old boots to wear. Such is life!'

* * *

Several unofficial evacuees lived in the village besides Chas. and James Mehegan, and Patricia and Jeanne Robinson. Anthony Hutchings,

10, and his brother Desmond, four, were from Plymouth but lived with their grandparents, Ernest and Eliza Ferris at Ford Cottages. On 1 May 1942, the head mistress Mrs Willis wrote in her teacher's journal: "Tony and Desmond Hutchings were very dirty. Their granny, Mrs Ferris, Ford Cottages, was warned by the nurse that they must be kept clean."

Several weeks later, on 5 May, Mrs Willis wrote: "Mrs Ferris has declared her intention of sending Tony Hutchings to Dunster School. I wrote to the Head Master there asking him to co-operate with her, even though in my mind this seems to violate school discipline."

Tony Hutchings returned to Timberscombe School a week later.

At Bickham Manor, William Gibbs Morell, the owner, took in 22 evacuees from Bristol in 1944. Morell was in the shipping business in Cardiff and in Minehead. He rented several cottages on the property to unofficial evacuees. Five-year-old Thomas Edward Vincent Craig and his brother, three-year-old Richard Vincent Craig, both lived in 2 Bickham Cottage but without either of their parents. It's likely their father, Terence Vincent Craig, who worked as a Lloyd's Underwriter, was a business associate of Mr Morel's.

Rita May Childs, 17, lived here too. She had come from the village in Hertfordshire where the Craig brothers lived. Their father, Terence Craig or Mr Morel, hired Gertrude Bayley, 42, as a certified nursery nurse. It's unknown whether any other small children lived at Bickham during this time.

Dorothy Cleverley from Greenford, Ealing, and her eight-year-old daughter Rosamond lived at Bickham, too, where Dorothy was employed as the cook.

★ ★ ★

The previous lives of evacuees and hosts had been starkly different. Evacuee mothers were not just bored and lonely and homesick. The day-to-day existence in the country was more simple and uncomplicated than it had been in the city. Many villagers were offended by their coarse behaviour and read it as bad manners and ingratitude.

At the start of the war, hosts in reception areas came to resent that parents were not required to pay anything towards the upkeep of their children. When parental contributions were introduced on 28 October 1939, the amount demanded did not cover the full billeting allowance paid to householders by the government. The rate ranged up to 6s. per child per week. Unemployed parents who received public assistance or were on meagre wages were not required to pay anything. Some parents subsidised the billeting allowance to foster parents, but others tried to avoid paying anything at all.

In *Exmoor in Wartime 1939-1945*, author Jack Hurley writes about two London school masters at Watchet who complained of 'almost open hostility by some foster parents toward the London school child. Insidious pressure, they said, was being applied to children so they would ask to be sent home. Some were kept outside their billets after school, even in wet weather and there were many other ways in which youngsters were being made miserable, said the masters.'

Not all evacuees came from poor areas. Some children found themselves evacuated from homes with bathrooms to billets that had no facilities, except a privy at the bottom of the garden and a tin bath in front of the fire.

Many evacuees had never experienced a loving home life in London. Here they saw how other mothers and fathers regarded each other, how brothers and sisters acted with each other. From the moment they arrived, local children gawked at them. Some evacuees started strategising about how to run away to London. For others, Timberscombe was as exotic as Africa. Endless fields and woodlands. Wildflowers, wild berries. Strange new foods – something called "soup". This was like stepping into another world.

5

"Women in Green"

Most evacuees didn't know how to react to life in the countryside. They had never laid eyes on a chicken or a pig, and that milk came from cows seemed preposterous. First impressions were guarded all around. WVS women who met them at railway stations were often as shocked as hosts were by some of the foul-mouthed, petulant children and mothers. They interpreted this kind of poverty as neglect.

Every hamlet and village had a WVS representative. They took on responsibility with posters for anti-gossip, collected aluminium pots and pans for salvage, and helped with new evacuee reception and billeting. Sometimes they had to remove evacuees from one household and place them somewhere else, which was often not a simple task. They removed a few cases of illnesses to hospital and formed evacuee clubs.

The Ministry of Supply asked that all WVS personnel assist local authorities in the salvage campaign. In every parish, salvage stewards encouraged every householder to do their part in the war effort by gathering paper, rags, string, bones, rubber, non-ferrous metals and old gramophone records.

Ada Trayhurn was the WVS centre organiser for Minehead and surrounding villages and hamlets, including Timberscombe. She and her husband, Jack, who was the head of English at Minehead Grammar School, lived in Dunster.

Like other WVS organisers, Mrs Trayhurn directed a housewives service – training of women in every street in first aid and anti-gas treatment. Mending service for the troops. Kitchen duties at the Minehead and West Somerset Hospital. Home Guard Feeding Scheme. They arranged for a blood transfusion service. Each WVS centre had its own Food Leader, who assisted the authorities in food rationing.

The WVS/WRVS Narrative Reports

At the end of each month, Ada Trayburn, like other WVS Centre organisers across the country, sent a report to headquarters in London. The report included brief statements about the activities of the centre during the month, under any of the following headings when appropriate:

(1) **EVACUATION**: (a) general position, numbers received and remaining; (b) residential units, i.e. sick bays, maternity homes, nursery centres, children's homes, hostels, etc.; (c) communal feeding; (d) clothing schemes; (e) leisure-time activities –adult, children; (f) any other activities

(2) **A.R.P. (Air Raid Precautions)**: including provision of shelter and amenities for the homeless after air raid.

(3) **TRANSPORT**

(4) **HOSPITAL SERVICES**: Including nursing auxiliaries, first aid lectures, blood transfusion service, etc.

(5) **CANTEENS**: (a) number of canteens; (b) authority under whom each canteen works; (c) number of helpers, paid/voluntary; (d) number fed per week; (e) type of food served

Other headings included: (6) **HOSPITAL SUPPLY DEPOTS AND WORK PARTIES**; (7) **MEETINGS**; and (8) **SALVAGE**.

Above: Women's Voluntary Services
(Ministry of Information Photo Division, Public Domain via Wikimedia Commons)

Excerpts from Mrs Trayburn's monthly reports

Minehead. December 1939.

Evacuees. About 80% remained before Christmas of original evacuees – these being almost entirely school children. Almost all the mothers have returned to London.

At the moment, the local authorities must reshuffle billets – at least 100 children are now awaiting the offer of new billets, their first householders have appealed for transfers – very few new billets have been offered, and the problem is becoming acute.

Residential unit – 2 hostels, the Polytechnic Boys School in Minehead, and a private house by Michael Hall School. One sick boy in a house also used for 'difficult' and 'backward' cases.

Maternity Home has been established and found to be of great usefulness to evacuee and local women.

Clothing Schemes. Private charity has given and distributed a large amount of clothing under the supervision of teachers. A local resident has mended boots and shoes where there is extreme necessity. Mending parties are attached to each evacuated school.

The scheme of collecting clothes through the British Legion or Evacuation Authority has been unsuccessful. Parents do not respond. Unemployment assistance has helped very few cases.

Leisure-time activities. Children's clubs have been set up at the Arcadia Hall in Minehead. Each evacuee child over the age of 11 years has at least one club a week. Children are escorted to and from the club in the black out.

A separate club for those billeted in Alcombe has been set up to meet once a week in the village hall. The local council has furnished equipment and board games.

In her reports, Mrs Trayburn doesn't mention a club of this sort being set up for evacuees in Timberscombe.

Some additional examples of her monthly reports:

Minehead. April 1940.
The number of evacuees remains about the same – 600. Special hostel is still used for troublesome cases. Play

clubs have been shut for summer months. Maternity Home is now being used for local cases and kept in readiness for any future evacuation.

Minehead. May 1940.
No additional evacuees have been received in Minehead and none are expected under the present evacuations arrangements. Evacuees continue as before. Some difficulty is found in re-billeting children where transfers have been applied for.

* * *

Though they had agreed to take in evacuees, some hosts turned them out-of-doors first thing in the morning, telling them not to return until evening. Some reports said the women "were filthy, and sometimes diseased; they were abusive, refused to be separated from their friends, and quite without manners or morals."

* * *

Within a few weeks of the outbreak of war – which people called the 'Phoney War' – many mothers and children had left the countryside and returned to their extended families. The bombing campaign had failed to materialise.

By early 1940, around 80% had returned home. But by the following summer, another wave of evacuations took place after Hitler invaded France and the launch of the Blitz.

Minehead. September 1940.
Besides the 600 evacuees who have remained in Minehead during the past year, additional groups have been received – about 60 from the bombed areas of London,

and 250 from Hastings. Five parties amounting to 1000 were accommodated in local halls for one night – 250 were later billeted in Minehead and the rest were sent to the adjacent rural areas.

WVS assisted the local authorities in all these arrangements and are still engaged in the furnishing of empty houses for evacuees. WVS members also provided transport for evacuees and brought food from storage under the direction of the Public Assistance Office.

Minehead. October 1940.
Evacuation Clothing Scheme. The central clothing depot at Minehead has received generous gifts from the American Red Cross – and Ministry of Health. We have sent proportions of these gifts to Williton and Watchet areas. Clothing has been distributed in Minehead to children of the evacuated school (West Ham) and to adults. Layettes have been sent to the evacuee maternity home, as well as individual mothers.

Minehead. February 1941.
The weekly meeting of evacuee women for sewing and social intercourse continues and serves a very useful purpose.

Minehead. March 1941.
The billeting officer sends a weekly list of new arrivals to the organiser. A WVS member who endeavours to smooth out difficulties visits each one, gives necessary information, and reports cases of genuine need – which are dealt with from the clothing depot.

Minehead. January 1942.
A steady stream of evacuees heads back to their homes.

Help has been given with clothing. Work parties formed for sewing and mending.

Minehead. December 1942.

Social club continues with nursery play room and classes for "Make and Mend" – Toy making. Christmas party for all evacuee mothers and children under 5 years.

Minehead. January 1943.

Social Club has re-opened after closing for Christmas. Attendance has dropped, owing to evacuees leaving the town to go home.

One of the biggest worries is that we cannot get the housewives – of who there are around 30 – to take any form of training. We have tried, but all in vain. And the number has not altered. Members must be cajoled into taking the simplest form of training and I should be very glad for any suggestions.

The collecting of salvage is going well and hope in time to get it much better. People are becoming very salvage-minded, also we are having offers of help from the most unexpected people.

We are anxious about boys' and girls' warm clothing, especially suits for boys and overcoats for boys and girls (ages 5-13 yrs). We have several women with their families in Watchet. It is tragic to see them so barely clad in this wintry weather.

Minehead. February 1943.

Social club now includes "Make and Mend" under instruction of a trained domestic social science teacher.

Additional Minehead WVS activities listed in 1943 were:
Clothing depot, ARP telephones, Forces mending services, assistance
at Toff Service Canteen VCPO, "Rural Pie" Transport, bandaging
practices and first aid exercises, making camouflaging nets. Collection
of rose hips and other wild herbs, which were dried at three stations
set up across the county.

Minehead. January 1944.

No rubber boots or prams have been received and no
toys for the nurseries mentioned in my last reports. The
children in all nurseries had a very happy Christmas.
Many parties were given for them and the staff. The
American Army visit in homes and is entertained. Gave
a wonderful party for the school children of Williton,
Watchet, and St Audries.

Few children, Mrs Trayburn wrote, were remembered by parents.

6

The Timberscombe School

On 30 September 1935, the new teacher recorded in the school journal: 'I, Kathleen A. Willis, began my duties as Headmistress today.'

In a short time, villagers saw that Mrs Willis was everything they could wish for in a schoolteacher. She was diligent, disciplined, and she kept the education and welfare of the pupils in her classroom foremost in her mind. Each one mattered to her.

Kathleen Willis was born in Minehead in Bampton Street in 1904, the daughter of a milkman. When she became headmistress, she and her husband, Bill Willis, and their two-year-old son Michael moved

Above: Timberscombe School Headmistress Mrs Kathleen Willis

Above: The school house cottage

into the schoolhouse cottage, adjacent to the school. Previously, they lived in Tiverton, where she had been school mistress. Just four months into the war, her father died. During the war years, she took off only one day to attend his funeral.

In her early years as headmistress, she wrote detailed descriptions of each student in the journal, their intellectual progresses, and their moral and spiritual growth. Once war was declared, the number of students in her classroom doubled overnight – from 35 to 70. Though she didn't object, it's clear from her journal entries that these evacuees were 'add-ons' she was obliged to include. Years later, none of the evacuees remember her losing her temper or ever being unkind. She was a pro.

Mrs Willis soon discovered these children had little or no education, no manners, and morals that were spotty. They brought bad habits and coarse language with them that the locals weren't used to. Occasionally,

INSTRUCTIONS.

1. The number of attendances missed by any scholar in any week must be entered in BLACK INK by the Head Teacher in the upper space opposite the child's name. No entry need be made if an attendance has not been missed.
2. The reasons for absence, ascertained by the Head Teacher from this Absentee Form or notes sent from parents, MUST be inserted in BLACK INK by the Head Teacher in the lower space opposite the child's name in accordance with the key.
3. The Attendance Officer will visit the parents of all children who have been absent, and in respect of whom no satisfactory explanation has been entered by the Head Teacher in this form. He will also visit the parents of scholars whose absence has been entered by the Head Teacher in this form on two successive weeks by the letter U or letter S, if no medical certificate has been received. In every case the action taken by the Attendance Officer MUST be entered in RED INK in the lower space, opposite the child's name, in accordance with the key.
4. This form must be made up and forwarded by the Head Teacher to the School Attendance Officer without fail at the close of the last school session in each week.

KEY TO REMARKS.

No.	NAME OF CHILD (Surname First)	NAME OF PARENT or GUARDIAN	ADDRESS (To be as full as possible)	D. of B.
1	Sparkes Annie	Mrs. Yandle	"Rosslyn" Cowbridge	4.3.26
2	Roach Ena	"	" "	23.3.26
3	Smith Iris	Lady Ryder	"Knowle" Dunster	10.9.26
4	Oliver Iris	Mrs Cleatworthy	"The Gardens" Timberscombe	29.10.26
5	White Dorothy	Lady Ryder	"Knowle" Dunster	23.3.27
6	Talbot Eunice	Mrs Coles	Combe Hse	26.4.27
7	Lawrence Elsie	Mrs Norman	Berrowcote Timberscombe	2.5.27
8	Munson Grace	Mr R Baker	Church St.	30.5.27
9	Smith Edna	Mrs Norman	Berrowcote	24.6.27
10	Robinson Joyce	Lady Ryder	"Knowle" Dunster	18.11.27
11				
12	Munson Iris	Mr R Baker	Church St, Timberscombe	2.8.29
13	Talbot Margaret	Mrs Brewer	Sunnyside	14.8.30
14	White Joan	Lady Ryder	"Knowle" Dunster	29.9.30
15				
16	Dedman Ronald	Miss D Huxtable	3 New Council Hses Timberscombe	15.10.25
17	Robinson Ernest	Lady Ryder	"Knowle" Dunster	22.11.25
18	Sutton Peter	Mrs Bryan	Brook House Timberscombe	12.2.26
19	Elton Fred	Mrs Elford	Ford Cott. "	4.4.26
20	Wells Fred	Mrs Ferris	" "	14.4.26
21	Sutton John	Mrs Ferris	The Square "	6.10.27
22	Oliver Arthur	Mrs Cane	Brook St. "	30.10.28
23	Smith Harry	Lady Ryder	"Knowle" Dunster	2.4.29
24	Robinson Thomas	"	" "	15.10.29
25	Sutton Norman	Mrs Slade	The Square, Timberscombe	29.3.30
26	Elton John	Mrs Elford	Ford Cott. "	20.3.31
27	Munson Ernest	Mrs Veale	Hill View "	30.9.31
28	Robinson Wm	Lady Ryder	Knowle Dunster	30.9.31
29	Smith Rapson	"	" "	10.10.31
30	Sutton Adrian	Mrs Bryan	Brook House Timberscombe	14.5.33
31	Smith Raymond	Lady Ryder	Knowle Dunster	16.12.33
32	Munson Sydney	Mrs Veale	Hill View Timberscombe	11.2.34
33	Robinson James	Lady Ryder	Knowle Dunster	1.4.34
34	Talbot Evelyn	Mrs Brewer	Sunnyside Timberscombe	30.1.32
35	White Iris	Lady Ryder	Knowle Dunster	20.3.33
36	Lambert Wm	Mrs Lambert	" "	13.9.33
37	Hadlow George	" Hadlow	6 Council Houses	31.3.33
38	Denwood John	Mrs Bowles	Knowle Dunster	23.6.32
39	Gibbs Doreen	Mrs Ray	Mill House Timberscombe	3.2.33
40				

Above: Timberscombe School evacuee roster (1939)
(courtesy of St. Petrock's History Group)

she acted as referee – not only between local children and evacuees, but between children, parents and hosts.

Each school unit leaving London was kept intact as much as possible, with the headteacher continuing to be in charge. Though many teachers had been evacuated, finding classroom space for them was problematic. Sometimes, merging evacuees and local students worked out and sometimes not. Cicely Elaine Cooper, the teacher at the Allerford School, describes her first morning in her memoir, *Memories of Selworthy and West Somerset.*

"I approached the school door confidently to hear an uproar going on in the porch. Violent cockney abuse was being hurled at some irate teacher, and the door flew open and out was thrust a strong arm clutching the back of the neck of a struggling, kicking mass of boyhood which collapsed on the floor and howled.

"Normal children only go berserk like animals when badly frightened. What was frightening them? Certainly not the Managers nor the people of Allerford.

"It was the uprooting, shaking away of all familiar contacts and habits, fear of the Blitz at home and then being left in charge of a teacher divested of the surroundings and authority of a big London school.

"I will not say that the evacuees and the natives ever came to love each other. My impression is that strangers are resolutely shut out from the West Countryman's understanding."

★ ★ ★

With 21,000 children arriving in Somerset, the county's school population increased by 50%. The Somerset County Education Commission attempted to split lessons between morning and afternoon shifts, at least in the beginning. Holidays were staggered, too. Local children had the usual fortnight for Christmas, but evacuees continued lessons up to Christmas Day.

In addition to the children removed by the government scheme, arrangements had to be made for the 3,000 who entered the county unofficially.

Separate communal meals were considered for the evacuees, though that plan became impractical. Two school nurses came from the London County Council, and three came from West Ham Educational Authority. Evacuees would need medical treatment, dental check-ups, clothing and travelling expenses. Out-of-school activities, with opportunities for handiwork, had to be set up. So did sick bays and hostels, and a nursery committee.

The evacuation scheme was never static but always changing, children changing billets; children and mothers departing and then returning some months later – a lot of coming and going. It became more of a logistical challenge than authorities could keep up with.

In *Exmoor in Wartime*, Jack Hurley writes that almost at once, a billeting tribunal at Minehead considered 35 complaints from householders about the conduct and habits of evacuees. Half of the complaints related to adults. Billeters were distressed by the shabby conditions of the children's clothes. Some of them organised jumble sales to meet the clothing needs.

Thomas Robinson

'*We went to school in the village which was 3/4 of a mile away, including a steep hill at Cowbridge, which included a blacksmith near the top.*

'*Mrs Willis used to cycle to Dunster to see her sergeant husband, where he was billeted. She was a lovely lady and well-liked, I'm sure. Mr Hadlow was from Essex. Mr Spink came with us from London. He was an excellent teacher.*'

At first, Mrs Willis arranged for the evacuees' classes to be held in the Reading Room.

'*We went to school in the morning, came home for lunch 'main meal', rushing our meal. Us older ones had to wash and wipe up and rush back to school in about 1 ½ hours.*

'One time, there was a plane noise with a rat-a-tat-tat of machine gun fire overhead. We were in school. Most of us Londoners ran to the windows to see a Spitfire chasing a German bomber which unloaded a bomb on the Exmoor hills, but it was shot down. The local children dived under their desks, as they had probably rehearsed.'

Norman Sutton

'Mrs Willis was an outstanding teacher. Mr Holland could be quick to use his hand on the boys. Jack always had trouble with the "th" sound. Mr Holland would say "thunder" and when Jack would try to repeat, he'd say "sunder". When he did, Mr Holland would give him a clap on the back of his head.'

'Mr Holland liked to use the cane. He was a vicious teacher. Some thought he must be a German spy.'

Maurice Huxtable

'Mrs Willis was strict. She took no nonsense. Hadlow came with the evacuees from West Ham, but he taught the locals too. He was easier.'

'At first, we went to school in the morning and the evacuees went in the afternoon. There were several of them at Knowle. One they used to push to school in a wheelchair. He was a little tiny boy, he was a dwarf. At one time, he was on the television, the circus, I believe. Roy Smith. They called him "Colonel".'

Roy Smith

'I got into trouble in the school when another boy was taking the piss out of me. I jumped up on top of the desk, grabbed the window cord and tied it round his neck, twisting it like a garrotte. If the teacher, Mrs Willis, hadn't stopped me, I would have killed him.'

Eddie Gande

'I started going to school in Timberscombe. Going in the morning was all right, but tough on the way home because it was all uphill. I went there for a year until we moved to Luccombe.

'I remember that the school was crowded. The teacher could handle only so many people. There were ages from five to 13 in one classroom. One boy from a farm came to school with ringworms. His desk had to be fumigated.

'Actual education in school was lacking for the small ones. We went on nature walks and picked foxgloves and rose hips.'

Ernie Munson

Mrs Willis and Miss Land were the local teachers. Mr Hadlow came from West Ham and Miss Fisher also came down from London. Boys and girls had separate playgrounds.

'The vicarage was across from the school. Rev Newman, the vicar, was a big fellow. He came into school once a week to give us religious education.

'One other item of my time at school in Timberscombe is (and how could I ever forget them) school dinners. They were cooked (I use the term loosely) in the kitchens at Dunster, they were put in large metal containers and delivered to the schools in the area, by the time we were sat down to the meal, they were lukewarm. I suppose the diet was as varied as could be, but it seemed like meat and two veg most days. There was a sweet of some kind: rice, tapioca or semolina. Those families of the children that had the dinners had to pay towards the cost, and if I remember rightly, it was 2s and 6p, which we took to school every Monday morning.

'The kitchens where the meals were cooked were at the back of the old police station, which is at the bottom of Dunster steep, about a hundred yards towards Minehead on the right, a big stone built place. It was said to be haunted.'

Brian Lambert

'My brother Billy and sister Jean went to the village school. I would go with my mother at lunchtime to take them a hot meal. To keep it warm, my mother would wrap a towel around it.'

Brian started to school in September 1941.

'I didn't learn to read or write and was only aware of one teacher, Mrs Willis. We were all in one room. The first year, I sat on the floor in front *and played all day; the second lot of children sat on chairs and were given lessons; and the older children had desks at the rear of the room and were also taught by Mrs Willis.*

'The little ones would be taken out on walks a lot.

'If any of the first-year children had a parent who could help, they would come and take us out for a walk around the country lanes. The only thing I learnt during my school time was to sing 'All Things Bright and Beautiful'.

Patricia Robinson

"The authorities decided that as Jeanne and I weren't official evacuees, we should attend school with the village children," she writes. "Soon we became friends. The schoolhouse was built in the 1800s and had a turreted bell, and I got to school early as I was allowed to ring it. We had lessons in the morning and nature rambles or country dancing in the Reading Room in the afternoon; and the London evacuees, vice versa."

★ ★ ★

The children were required to carry gas masks to school and then home again. During drills, students practiced putting on masks at a moment's notice. In air raid warning drills, they were instructed to run to school or back home, if they were outside, depending on which was nearer. If they had a two or three mile trek across fields and they were isolated, they were told to put on gas masks and lie under a hedge.

★ ★ ★

On 1 Sept 1939, Mrs Willis wrote in the teacher's journal: 'Owing to the Evacuation of London school children, the school was closed today until further notice.'

On the 11th, school was reopened for local children and a week later, on the 18th, a double shift began. Local children attended from 8:00 to 2:00 in the schoolhouse. Evacuated children attended from 1:00 to 5:00 in the Reading Room or out of doors. Teachers who accompanied evacuees from London were in charge of that group. By November the 20th, the morning sessions were 8:30 to 12:30 (4 hours) and the afternoon sessions were 1:30 to 2:30 in the Reading Room or out of doors.

By December, the daily schedule still needed some ironing out. The Somerset Chief Education Officer, WJ Deacon, suggested a readjustment. Morning sessions should be 8:45 to 12:15 and afternoon sessions from 1:30 to 2:30 for both local children and evacuees. This allowed 4 ½ hrs. of instruction daily.

By early 1940, evacuee students had regular Reading Room furniture, but it was not equipped with desks or other classroom furniture that were supposed to have arrived from London. West Ham Infants were merged with Timberscombe Infants. The remaining teacher took charge of the rest of the West Ham children.

By the third week of April, no furniture had been received for the room. Mr Hadlow, the West Ham teacher, registered the evacuee students in a separate block on the local students' register.

Dr Stirling carried out a medical inspection at the school, and there was also a dental examination. Fourteen local children and evacuees were treated.

That June, the Diocesan Inspector arrived and gave Mrs Willis and her students a report that put a good face on the situation:

> There is a pleasant and wholesome atmosphere about the prayers and singing, and it is plain that the teachers aim to provide all the children with a suitable and helpful religious upbringing. The presence of strangers is not unwelcome. The readiness of the town children helps the others to get the better of their natural slowness of thought and speech, and adds to the brightness of the

Infant Group. Here there is a good foundation of simple knowledge, on the whole well shared, and memory work is praiseworthy.

In the Upper Group, sound, sufficient and definite instruction has been given, book work and subject matter are on the whole known and laid to heart, and painstakingly reproduced. There is also some show of expression in the written work. Difficulties have been overcome, and good use made of opportunities, and the school is on the whole reported Good all round.

Diocesan Inspector W. Gedge
Received June 19th 1940

Though classroom furniture had arrived over the summer, when school reopened in September 1940, the County Education Office suggested the merging of the Gainsborough Road West Ham evacuees with Timberscombe students and the closing of the Reading Room. Mr Hadlow brought in 24 evacuees and from then on, would be Mrs Willis's assistant teacher. Along with 43 local children, seven new evacuees arrived and there were now 74 children in the single classroom.

Mrs Willis attempted to bring order to this new arrangement by designating Miss Land as teacher for Infants to 8+. As head teacher, she would be in charge of the 9-11+ year olds, and Mr Hadlow would take the 12-14+ year olds.

By the end of October 1940, when school closed for Half Term, evacuees were given a full week off. Mr Hadlow, she wrote, was ill and absent the last day. When school reopened five days later, he was still absent, suffering from ear trouble. When the evacuee children returned several days later, Mr Hadlow was still absent and Mrs Willis noted that she had requested a supply teacher to fill in.

Mr Holland was transferred from Minehead to assist. Without

notice, Mr Hadlow returned a month later and discovered Mr Holland had taken his place, so he left. Mr Holland became Mrs Willis's permanent assistant.

Meanwhile, more evacuees were being admitted, nine from Kent, several from the LCC.

Before long, Mr Holland was absent without leave, and Mrs Willis reported his unsatisfactory behaviour to the Education Committee. Mr Nolan, another West Ham teacher who was teaching in Alcombe, was sent to replace him.

Frank Ford, the constable in Timberscombe, called to ask if Mrs Willis knew of Mr Holland's whereabouts. A warrant had been issued for his arrest.

Police officers in Minehead issued arrest warrants to anyone who was out after curfew, and maybe this had happened to Mr Holland. He might have been in Minehead, sitting in jail rather than teaching school.

In March 1941, Mrs Willis lost Mr Nolan, who was transferred to Watchet. Miss King returned to the Dunster school and after the Easter holidays, Mr Dobinson was sent from West Ham.

In March, Mrs Willis recorded: Somerset 43, West Ham 14, Bristol, 7, Plymouth 1, Southampton 1, Cardiff 1, Kent 2, L.C.C. 4, for a total of 73.

In May of 1941, twenty school children from Bristol were evacuated and likely went to live at Bickham Manor. Their teacher, Miss Sybil M Mould, taught classes in the vicarage kitchen.

Miss Mould, a 33-year-old domestic science teacher from Bath, accompanied evacuees from Bristol to teach cookery, sewing and other household skills. In North Somerset, she had also been an ARP (air raid precautions). She may have continued these duties in Timberscombe, or at least passed along the knowledge to students. ARP wardens patrolled the streets during blackout, to ensure that no light was visible. If a light was spotted, the warden would alert the person/people responsible.

Upon inspection that July, County Education Inspectors found the vicarage kitchen unsuitable as a classroom and suggested reorganising the local school to incorporate Bristol children. She suggested the vicarage was very damp and unfit for Infants. From then on, Miss Land used the kitchen occasionally for activities. Lessons were to be held outdoors as much as possible. If the weather was wet, all three classes would work in the main room.

In early July, the number on the rolls was 54 from Somerset, 22 from West Ham, and 20 from Bristol, for a total of 96.

Enrolment numbers were always fluctuating. In September, when the school reopened, the number was 86. Mrs Willis was headmistress, Miss Land taught Infants. Miss Mould taught the Lower Juniors, and Mr Dobinson taught the Upper ages.

Then in September, HMI Matthews visited and disapproved of the present arrangement of three classes and three teachers in the main room. He suggested the hire of an extra room for the Infants, and the other two groups would remain in the main room. There should also be a floating teacher.

Mrs Willis and the inspector examined the skittle alley at the pub as a possible extra classroom. After Christmas, it might have to be used if the Reading Room (now in military hands) was unavailable.

In 1941, evacuee children, as well as local children, were candidates for the County Free Peace Scholarship. 'The exam was held in the classroom today,' Mrs Willis wrote. 'Beryl Pike (from Bristol), William Robinson, John Elton (West Ham Junior) Iris Munson (West Ham Senior). Invigilators. Rev R. Newman–correspondent. Mr J Land–manager.'

On 14 June 1942, Assistant Diocesan Inspector Rev G.V. Yonge conducted a Scripture Examination. Undoubtedly, Yonge's language hit all the right notes and must have pleased his supervisors as well as the Somerset Education Committee.

> This happy school left an exceedingly favourable impression upon the Inspector, as of a place where religion was not a school subject but rather the basis of the school.

The children themselves, having several opportunities to sing, take their full share of the opening prayers. A school like this should be a true nursery of Church men and women, carrying out as it seems to do the intention of its 18th century founder as far as is humanly possible. Here, too music is made the Handmaid of the Church....
A church school in the full meaning of the word.

Besides admissions, Mrs Willis recorded the dates when evacuees left and when some of them returned. In 1943, 14 March, she wrote: '7 children have left number on roll to be 58. 3 Fregido. G. A. P., 2 Gande M.E., 2 Aden Raymond and D. and Gregory.' And later that month, she wrote, 'John Elton, 14 Cliff St. Canning Town has returned home.'

25 January 1944. 'The County Psychologist came to examine Tony Pring (Bristol Evacuee).'

4 February 1944. 'Raymond Smith, Roy Smith, West Ham evacuees, and Sheila Pring and her brother Tony were removed from Knowle. Tony Pring was removed to a hostel in Taunton while Sheila returned to Bristol.'

15 February 1944. 'Owing to a fire destroying the Timberscombe Reading Room, the following furniture which was stored there was destroyed. An 8-year-old boy named George Milton, who lived in The Great House, lit a hay rick nearby, which then engulfed the Reading Room. Lost were 13 dual desks from Bristol, 4 dual desks from West Ham, and 6 dual desks from Somerset.'

The school closed for Victory Days, 8-9 May 1945, in celebration of Victory in Europe. On 19 December 1945, the following furniture was returned by G.W.R. (Carries, Burrell) to Manor Road School, West Ham: 6 small dual desks, 10 small chairs, 1 teacher's desk, and 1 easel. When the Wootton Courtenay School closed down in September 1946, followed by the Luccombe School in June 1947, those students were added to the roster at Timberscombe School. By then, most evacuees that would return to London had left.

7

The Ladies

After the Great War, the three Ryder sisters became the most formidable family in Timberscombe. They were daughters of the 4th Earl of Harrowby in Staffordshire. Since male heirs inherited the estate, Lady Margaret and Lady Constance went west to Somerset and made Knowle Manor their residence in 1919. Their younger sister, Lady Audrey Anson, the only daughter who married, became a widow in 1924 and joined them at Knowle, where she lived for the rest of her life.

The manor house was an Elizabethan style country house c. 1878, built of red sandstone, with a steeply pitched slate roof, decorative ridge tiles, obelisk finials to gabled end bays and a three-storey central

Above: Knowle Manor (photograph by R. Kingsley Taylor)

Above left: Lady Audrey Anson
Above right: Lady Constance Ryder

porch. After Lady Margaret died in 1932, Lady Constance and Lady Audrey carried on as benefactors to the village and villagers and continued the Ryder tradition of Good Works.

Lady Constance was 68 at the beginning of the war and Lady Audrey was four years younger. 'They were like chalk and cheese,' John Munson says. John lives in Minehead and is the youngest sibling of one of the evacuee families. 'Constance was larger than life, sturdy. I think of her in tweeds. Audrey always wore a black coat like she was in mourning. She was a beanpole. Both were very organised. Regimented with their lives.'

Constance was a manager for the Timberscombe School, a Church Warden, church organist and choir director. She was a Justice of the Peace in Minehead. The Ladies had been active in Scouting at

Harrowby. Lady Constance became Commissioner of the Boy Scouts in the West Country and Lady Audrey Commissioner of the Girl Guides. The Ladies brought structure to their adopted part of West Somerset. By the time the evacuees arrived, the sisters controlled the village.

Thomas Robinson

'The ladies were religious, Church of England. They took us to Sunday School. Lady Ryder donated the organ from their estate in Harrowby to St Petrock's and dedicated it to her brother, who had died in the war. She played it every Sunday, using an old air pump.

'In my third year, at 13 years old, I was head choirboy. We had choir practice at the church and at Knowle. I was patrol leader in the Scouts – I knew my knots. We built a raft and took it out onto the pond, and it stayed up. We went waste paper collecting for the war effort, going to outlying farms.

'The ladies always came in at dinner time midday and made sure we ate all our food, and they always came in our bedrooms late at night and tucked us in. Usually, we were asleep. We were strictly brought up. Some of the other evacuees who lived with the villagers had a lot more freedom, and a bit more loving parents, but I do not regret my time there, apart from being away from my loving parents and other siblings.

Tom remembers the three sisters from Dagenham, Dorothy, Iris and Joan White. At that time, Dagenham was said to be the most poverty-stricken borough in London. He recalls the Smith family, especially Roy Smith, the youngest, who was a dwarf, and Harry, the oldest, who he says: 'caused trouble and was 'a bit of a lad'.

Later in the war, six-year-old Harry Dale arrived from Bristol to live at Knowle.

'He was nervous, shell-shocked. We saw others from West Ham at the school. Some were homesick. A few returned to London. My brother and sisters and I were well looked after. The ladies took good care of us.'

Above: Lady Constance Ryder and Scouts

Above: Lady Audrey Anson and Girl Guides

Roy Smith

'Lady Constance ran the Wolf Cubs and the Boy Scouts; and Lady Audrey ran the Brownies and the Girl Guides, which all of us were a part of, along with the children in the village.

Lady Audrey made us laugh because she used to fart a lot, and every time she did, she gave a little cough to hide it. Anyway, they asked me to join the Cubs and kitted me out with a uniform, a green jumper and a beret and with a scarf and a woggle, and they made me sort of sergeant because I could recite the alphabet backwards, which nobody else could. I already knew deaf and dumb language, the Morse code and semaphore, which my Mum had taught me. My Mum was very clever, and had also taught me shorthand – not Gregg's or Pitman's but gypsy shorthand, writing backwards and so then Lady Constance wanted me to teach all these things to the other Cubs and Scouts.

'I also showed them how to make a raft. Then I taught them tracking, which is another thing that gypsies are very good at, using sticks and stones to lay a trail.

'One time, I made a raft across the river with this other boy, Harry Dale, who came from Bristol. Now when you are a Boy Scout, or at least in those days, you always had to have what they called a staff or a stave. I used that to stick in the water and steer the raft across the river. Harry tried to cross the river without a stave and got stuck halfway. I was on the bank and said, 'I'll give you a push' and pushed him right in. He was always moaning, that Harry Dale. 'Everyone's always having a go at me,' he used to say, which was true, because we were kids, and that day I did. He fell right in. 'I can't swim' he said, so I said: 'Drown!' but we pulled him out in the end and you can guess who got the blame.

'Mum and Dad used to come visit, but they had to stay in Watchet. The two Ladies used to send their chauffeur over there to pick them up. I remember walking up the drive to the house to meet my parents after not having seen them for a long time. We were all dressed up in our Cubs and Boy Scout uniforms, and you can imagine what I looked like with my little legs, wearing short trousers, my woggle and my scarf, with the badges down the jumper.

My Mum couldn't get over it. She had to laugh when I went up to her and saluted her with my three fingers to my forehead. Then Mum started tears again and crying and I said, 'I want to come home, I want to come home'.

'And then I did a very naughty thing. Lady Constance had let me have a pony and trap, which I used to take around the village collecting wastepaper and cardboard that was sold to a scrap merchant to raise money for the Cubs and Scouts. One weekend, I picked up a good load, sold it for £6 10s – and kept the money. Lady Constance called all the Cubs and the Scouts together on the lawn in front of the house, dressed me down in front of them like a court martial, and then snipped off all my badges with a pair of scissors, with me crying buckets and feeling so ashamed of myself.

'It was humiliating, but I wouldn't blame her for it. She was wonderful to me, really, and I think she loved me, in some sort of way. Years later, not so long ago, I was waiting to go into Court at Bow Street for some minor little thing, causing an obstruction, and a woman comes up to me and says, "Are you Royston?" It was her niece who I'd known as a child. The family still remembered me, forty years later.'

Norman Sutton

Norman lived with the Slades in Holes Square, but he remembers spending a good part of his time at Knowle for choir practice and Boy Scouts.

'Lady Ryder gave us 1p per service, day and night, and also a pence for choir practice. We made 3p a week. I'd go to Loveridge's to buy Herbie Slade's cigarettes, Kensitas, because they came in a pack of 20 + 4 extras. While I was there, I'd buy cigarettes for myself, too, using the choir money from Lady Ryder.

'At Christmas, we went carol singing around the different houses. We became a part of the community.'

Ernie Munson

'Constance Ryder had most to do with the boys. We all became choir boys at St Petrock's. Twelve to fifteen boys. Audrey didn't have much to do with us. '

Local boys were likely members of the choir too, he says, but he remembers them all being evacuees.

'On Sundays, Lady Constance made us go to service, Sunday school, then evensong. Then we'd all walk back. Whenever the two sisters talked about something they didn't want the boys to know about, they spoke in fluent French.'

Roy Smith

'When I was taken ill at Knowle, Lady Constance was very kind to me. She found me lying on the Chesterfield, doubled up in pain, and called the district nurse, Nurse Leigh. 'He's in a bad way,' said Lady Constance, who then called Bolsie, who was her chauffeur and her gamekeeper, and drove her around in one of those big Austin limousines, and they laid me out on the back seat of the car and drove me into Minehead hospital where the doctors operated on me straight away. It was peritonitis.

'This was 1942 or 1943, long before the National Health Service started. It was private medicine in those days, and Lady Constance paid all the bills while I was in there, and she visited me regularly. She used to bring me fruit juice and fresh apples and pears from her orchard, making quite a fuss of me. The war seemed very far away. It never occurred to me that Mum and Dad might still be in danger in West Ham until one night, during a blackout, we looked through the hospital windows and saw British and German fighters in aerial combat, having a dog-fight.'

Eddie Gande

'We had to move out of our quarters at Knowle Farm and go to a bungalow on Knowle Lane, the back road. Mrs Lambert and her children were going to Dunster and stopped by to see Mum. When she left us, she was pushing the pram down the road with Brian in it. Jean walked along beside her. Billy was on his scooter, and then there was the accident. That affected every one of us in some way, the evacuees and the locals.

'We stayed in the Bungalow for about six months after that. Then a worker on the farm and his family wanted it, so they moved us up to

Croydon Farm. That March of 1942, our father was on leave and came to see us. That's when Mum got pregnant with Jackie.

Ernie Munson

'My parents had come down. My father was treated for his back and worked for Frank Huxtable. We had quarters over the stables. Four bedrooms, a living room, and the kitchen with a paraffin stove.

'The Ladies had pedigree Jersey cows, shire horses and a vegetable garden with a full-time gardener. Mom worked when they needed help to get potatoes in out of the fields. All the staff helped.

'The housekeeper and the butler would keep tabs on us. The butler, Mr Mees, hit a two-foot wide gong when dinner was ready. Mrs Chipling was the cook. Large like on the TV series Upstairs Downstairs *or* Downton Abbey. *She wore a long white starched apron. We would help. We had to scrub the kitchen table. Occasionally, she would give us biscuits.*

'An evacuee named Harry Dale, who was from Bristol, lived there with me and Sid in a dorm room in the big house.

'Roy Smith was a proper little cockney. Years later, he married a showgirl. She was tall, legs up to her armpits. A picture of them was in the newspaper, walking down the street in London, holding hands.

'I don't know if they were gypsies or travellers, like he said. He would get us into trouble.'

Brian Lambert

To this day, the accident that took his brother Billy's life comes back to Brian in fragments. Like in a dream. He knows this hodge-podge memory is true because his mother and sister Jean filled in the details for him over the years. He remembers how Billy was with them one day and then one day he wasn't.

Other than his brother's accident, Brian only remembers bits of the earlier days at Knowle.

'Climbing a haystack, falling off, getting a mild concussion. Running down a stone pathway from the farm to the big house and ran into a wall.

'The Ladies owned Knowle, but they didn't do much for us. We were on our own. Once they brought some windfall apples so my mother could make a pie but they were all wormy. Sometimes we got rabbits from them.'

* * *

In July 1941, Ernie Munson's mother gave birth to a boy at Knowle. They named him David. He only survived four days. His brothers didn't know where he was buried until recently.

John Munson

'After a chance meeting with an old school mate some few months back, I found out that many years ago he acquired a diary belonging to the chap who dug the graves in Minehead during the war years. After looking through it, we found the site of our brother David's grave, so it was good news after 80 years of not knowing. I visited the plot, it was quite emotional.'

John Munson was born in the stable at Knowle Farm when the family lived there in 1944.

'Our father was quite involved with the Scouts at Knowle. He helped build the original Scout hut in the quadrangle and then the hut in a field above Cowbridge, up high, right behind the hedge. The Ladies presented him with a "thank you" badge.'

The light green hut still stands, though now it's overgrown with brambles and forest.

'Dad and my mother came down from London because of Dad's accident with his back. He was disabled, but he worked sometimes for Frank Huxtable, building coffins, hundreds of them. Shipped them off. He used to call them 'cheap and nasty' coffins.

'After we moved to Dunster in 1948 or '49, Dad would go to Knowle to see the Lady Constance and Lady Audrey. They were my godparents.

Roy Smith

'Our stay at Knowle came to an end soon after I came out of hospital.

Lady Constance and Lady Audrey were getting on in years. It was getting to where we were really more than they could handle. My brother Harry could go back home to West Ham because he was the eldest, but my brother Raymond and me were sent to live in a place called Crowcombe, which was also in Somerset, with me staying with this one couple; and Raymond staying with the woman's elderly widowed mother next door. Raymond couldn't suffer it because she was always telling him what time he had to be home. I wouldn't take no chat off the people I was staying with.'

John Munson
'Dad was still involved with Knowle when Lady Constance died. He helped take her body to the Midlands to be buried in the Ryder family tomb.'

8

Walter Copp

Each former evacuee singles out one person when asked about their memories of Timberscombe: Walter Copp. None of them had ever met a man so knowledgeable about music and the natural world. He could take a piece of wood and carve it into some recognisable form of life, like it might stir or take a breath. A few evacuees say now they knew Copp was unique, a renaissance man, though as children none of them could have defined what that meant. He introduced them to the night sky with his telescope. He showed them his insect, bird egg and butterfly collections, groups of objects that no boy from the End of London ever saw before. Even now, they think of their times with him as a privilege.

Walter Copp was born in Wootton Courtenay in 1889, the eldest child of John and Elizabeth Copp. His father, born in 1846, was an agricultural worker, just as past generations of men in his family had been. John Copp was 18 years older than Walter's mother.

Due to some unknown circumstances or events, Walter broke the mould. He apprenticed and had become a tailor by the time he and Bessie Stenner married at St Petrock's Church in 1915. They set up house in Timberscombe at 5 Bemberry Bank, next door to Bessie's family. He lived there until his death in March 1970, when he was 80 years old.

He was a school manager, along with Lady Constance Ryder, Mrs Alice St John Mildmay from The Great House, Lady Audrey Anson, Mr Land and Reverend Newman.

In later years, people in the village remember him sitting in the window at Hobb's, a tailor's shop in Dunster where he worked, one leg crossed over the other, all dressed up and looking like an advertisement for a suit he made. He also made trousers and corduroy britches, which most farmers on Exmoor wore.

Walter enlisted six months after his and Bessie's son Leonard was born. Their son, Cyril Copp, was born in 1918. Walter was discharged on 29 August 1919, from the Labour Corps in the British Army. Leonard died in 1922 of scarlet fever. He was five.

Where does someone with Walter Copp's outstanding talents and skills come from? His curiosity led him, and to a degree, he was self-taught. A woodcarver named Ernest William Pennington who lived over in West Hatch made carvings for All Saints in Wootten Courtenay and the church in Selworthy. He also taught wood carving. At an early age, it's likely that Walter was one of Ernest's students, as was his son Cyril. Later, Walter taught village boys in Timberscombe and the evacuees how to wood carve.

Above: Walter Copp
(courtesy of St. Petrock's History Group)

Ernie Munson

'Mr Copp played the organ on Sundays at All Saints in Wootton Courtney. Every week, he would take us out for the day on nature walks. He took us over Dunkery, pointing out different things. He knew where to find red deer. At night, we would gather around, and he would point out the stars. He taught us how to find the constellations, and what their names were, and the myths they were taken from. He had a collection of bird eggs. Copp was a grand chap who taught us about nature.'

Norman Sutton

'He would take groups out to the country, a half dozen at a time, and point out different birds and animals. He knew where to look for herds of red deer.

'He took a shine to my brother Peter and took him out to the countryside. Years after we left Timberscombe and were back in London, I would see a bird and Peter could identify it.

'One night a week, eight of us would go over to the Copp's house and he taught us to play hand bells. He was a bell-ringer at the church. He had sheet music for all of us and taught us how to read it. When we made tunes for him, or at church, it gave us a sense of achievement.

Patricia Robinson (Kiln Farm)

From her memoir: "Mr Copp was the tailor and had been responsible for some of the carving in the church. His son Cyril was in our class at the school and was later to marry Brenda Quartly."

Thomas Robinson

'He must have been a world traveller. He knew a lot of different things. They were an interesting family. He had a collection of butterflies from all over the world in a box.

'We'd go for walks over Dunkery Beacon. He could identify birds and taught us how. 'Once up on Exmoor hill, we saw two stags fighting down below. No kid from London had ever seen anything like that. I remember that time as clear as day.'

9

Mixing With the Locals

Ernie Munson remembers Frederick Norman because he was so tall, well over six feet, and stood upright when he read the verses at the church service on Remembrance Day. Fred was also one of the bell ringers. The Normans lived in Berrowcote, next to Frank and Eva Huxtable, and he tried to get Maurice Huxtable interested in bell-ringing. Maurice showed up on the practice night. He didn't like it and didn't mind saying so. He remembered Fred's response. 'Thank you, lad, for telling me the truth.'

When war broke out, Philip Isidore Lach-Szyrma was vicar at St Petrock's. He died early in 1940 and in February, Rowland Alan Webb Newman became the new vicar. Before coming to Timberscombe, Rev Newman had been chaplain at St Audries School for Girls.

St Audries was a converted mansion in West Quantoxhead. During the war, lorry loads of historic treasures, mainly from churches in London, were kept in its cellar and outbuildings. Carvings and stained glasses, fonts, pulpits, screens and other examples of ancient craftsmanship.

Rev Newman's wife, Fanny Aston, had died in May 1939. When he came to Timberscombe, it was with a new wife, Maureen Graham, who he had met as a nurse caring for his late wife at a nursing home in Greenwich. He had suffered from tuberculous arthritis in the elbow and his arm had been amputated. He and Maureen became guardians of a four-year-old evacuee named Sadie Samson. Upon leaving Timberscombe, Sadie left with him and, later, family members said that she was Newman's adopted daughter.

Thomas Robinson

'During my father's holiday, my parents came to see us every year in the summer for a week or two. I think they were pleased with what we learnt during our time at Timberscombe. I knew the Morse Code, semaphore, knots and splices, astronomy, farming, animal welfare, milking, feeding, cleaning, herding cows and sheep, gardening. A lot of which is now forgotten.

'We went rabbiting quite a bit. We had two ferrets and nets to cover some holes in the hedges. One hole was left open to put the ferret in and it drove the rabbits into the nets, which we captured. I sent one home once, but I didn't paunch it, so it was full of maggots when it got to London. I was only 13 but learnt my lesson.

'We didn't have a radio, so we couldn't listen to the news. The Ladies did not want us to hear about the bombing in London, but the other evacuees living in the village listened to the news and told us all about it. The only time we were told about the war was when Lady Ryder's nephew "Red Rider" took his submarine into a German port and planted bombs in the surrounding buildings. He got home with the loss of some of the crew. A film was made of his daring raid after the war.

'Above Timberscombe, on top of the hill, was a tree standing all by itself, a beech. I climbed to the top with a large white sheet and hung it on the top. It was noticed by someone, and the Home Guard was called out, thinking it was a German parachutist. I got into trouble for that.

'If anything happened a bit on the naughty side, it seemed we were blamed, probably more often true, I think. Sometimes the village policeman, Ford I think his name was, would tell us off if we were scrapping apples or for going into vegetable gardens. He had a son who was quite a lad with the girls.

'Once a chicken went missing from one of the farms. I used to cut across the fields to avoid the road on my way to school. I passed the farm and was blamed, accused of taking it. They found the chicken laying eggs in one of the hedges.

'A family of gypsies by the name of Holland lived up in Holes Square. Some lived in caravans in the fields. We earned money from them by picking whortleberries up on the hill and by selling rabbits.

'Jim Jeffrey, who owned the shop, lost his eye during the war and had a glass eye. He was 2nd in command of the Home Guard. He kept a lookout, but we still pinched a few things.'

Maurice Huxtable

Maurice remembers that Lance Percival, who would grow up to become the well-known actor, comedian and singer, was an evacuee and lived at Rosemont Cottage for a short time.

'We used to take the mickey out of him. Call him "Nance". 'My name's not Nance,' he'd say. He was… swanky.'

Chas Mehegem

'There was a boy taller than me who, as I remember, was always up for a lark. Invariably, his socks were always round his ankles. I suppose that was Lance.'

John Gratton

'Everything was rationed. Food was rationed. Clothes were rationed. Furniture was rationed. You couldn't get anything without a ration card, except if you went on the black market.

'Joycie went to school. I stayed home until I was five. Mother and Joycie got on very well. I can remember them sitting on either side of the fireplace, both knitting. It was quite a happy time, really.

'Joyce took a milk route up in Dunster. At the castle. The dairy was halfway up castle hill at Dairy Cottage. She had a handcart with little milk churns in it and ladles. And some milk in bottles. And she went around Dunster, pushing this handcart, dishing out milk into jugs. I used to go with her on a Saturday morning.'

Roy Smith

'We were still going to the village school at Timberscombe, and I got into trouble again. The first time was when a boy called Billy Robinson kept calling me 'dwarf' and taking the piss out of me. He said he wanted a fight,

so I took him down to the river. I pushed his head under the water, let him up, and then pushed him back under. 'You shouldn't have done that,' he said. 'That's your bleeding fault,' I told him. 'You shouldn't take liberties.' I've had that sort of trouble all my life, but you can only take so much.'

Norman Sutton

Often, Norman played cricket at the cricket field with the Huxtables. He helped Tommy Heard from the pub deliver newspapers in the van to small villages as far as Tarr Steps. On Church Street, past the church, he remembers a farmer named Frederick Norman, another Frederick Norman, not the man who was the bell ringer and lived at Berrowcote.

'Frederick Norman had a plum tree I would climb for him. He said, 'You can eat as many as you like.' And he paid me a few coppers. I knew the Slades would not be happy about that.'

Norman and his younger brother Adrian, who lived at the Bryans with Peter, their oldest brother, helped Louis Thorne at Great House Farm. They would help with haymaking and cutting corn. They cared for the shire horses, taking them to fields.

'We would have a ploughman's lunch, but without the cider, which the farmer wouldn't allow.

'Jimmy Jeffreys had a greenhouse up at the old abandoned quarry. That's where he grew his veg for his store. Eva Huxtable would give us empty baskets so we could go up and pick whortleberries she would sell. At Bickham, in the winter, Mr Morel would invite us to come sledge down the deep slope in front of his house.'

Norman remembers Notely Hosegood, the farmer who lived up at Aldercott, and how he spent all his time at the pub. Notley, he says, was inept at farming. He would ride his horse down to the village, leave it outside the Lion. When he'd had too much to drink, they would put him on the horse. The horse would take him home to the stable and dump him off in the hay where he'd stay until morning. He ended up losing the farm, Norman says.

Like the rest of England, people in Timberscombe were concerned about the food supply. Since Britain was an island, everyone knew that the country could be cut off by Germans so they couldn't rely on imports. They could only depend on the food they grew themselves in allotments.

As he remembers it, village boys kept separate from the evacuees – except through Scouts and the choir. And teasing Harold Hobbs.

Harold was a disabled man in his forties. He and his parents lived at 5 Council House, next door to the Birchams and one house away from Dudley and Grace Huxtable, Maurice's parents. Lady Constance hired him to pump the organ for morning and evening services every Sunday as she played. A plaque above the organ commemorates Harold for his service.

Norman recalls the boys taunting him.

"How do geese fly, Harold?" and Harold would flap his arms.'

Life in the Slades household was happy, but in time he became homesick. After a few years, he returned home for a holiday in summer. When he came back to Timberscombe, he missed his family more than ever. He wrote to his dad that he was going to run away. So his mother came to Timberscombe to get him and his brother Adrian to bring them back to London. Peter, who was older, had already returned.

Losing Adrian was a blow to Mrs Bryan. Many foster-mothers were kind to the evacuees they took in but kept indifferent. Elizabeth Bryan, 70, loved this child in her care and wanted to adopt him. By this time, she felt he belonged to her. When Mrs Sutton arrived in Timberscombe, she found a child who had become accustomed to another way of life. He had a foreign-sounding Somerset accent and affection from a substitute mother. Adrian's ties with the Bryans would remain strong, and he and Norman continued to visit them regularly.

★ ★ ★

In 1944, prior to the Allied army's invasion of the Continent, American troops in training descended on Exmoor by the thousands. Their tanks and armoured vehicles dwarfed the cottages. As June approached, more and more American troops in the last stages of invasion training spread over Exmoor and the Brendons. Two large camps were at Cannington and Dulverton. General Dwight D. Eisenhower, now supreme commander of the Allied Forces, had his headquarters in a trailer in a wood near Portismouth.

Thomas Robinson

'When we went paper collecting for the war effort, American GIs were stationed up the road going to the snowdrop field. They came into the village, courting some girls and going into shops.

'The American Army took over a farm about a mile from the village. I became friendly with a GI Sergeant, who often gave us peanut butter and sweets, but the young women in the village were given nylon stockings in kind, so to speak. They would give kids American stamps and envelopes.

'The Home Guard had been formed earlier. A Sergeant was in charge along with Ex-Corporal Jim Jeffrey, who owned the grocery and sweet shop, and had a glass eye. We used to watch them doing their thing. It was like Dad's Army, which I loved later on the telly. It was so true to life. Some were a little backward, so to speak, didn't know their left from their right.'

Maurice Huxtable

'There were so many American soldiers here, up on the hill, up toward Luxborough. They came into the village. Gave us sweets, called it "candy'.

'They had an enormous tower up there. Dug out up there, covered the pits with branches in case the Germans landed here. When D-Day came, they all disappeared.'

John Gratton

'In 1944, there were thousands of American GIs all around Dunster. They were camped at Dunster deer park. American troops everywhere. The lanes were filled with trucks and American troops.

'One of the great highlights of our day was standing at the bottom of

Dunster Steep and watching these convoys of troops going up over Dunster and us shouting out to them. They threw out oranges from the back of their lorries and chocolate bars for all the rest to grab. A great source of enjoyment, a great source of food, thanks to the Americans.'

Ernie Munson

'At the big house in Bickham, the American army took over. They'd drive their tanks down through the village, come around the corner and knock down corners of a wall at Huxtables. Come fix it the next day. Then knock it down again the next.'

Chas Mehegan

'A few miles from the village, there was an American army camp. There were stories that when they were ordered overseas, they buried lots of tinned food and clothing, which the villagers dug up as soon as they had left.'

Ernie Munson

'We got on all right with village boys. We spoke in a different way, had a Cockney accent. They couldn't understand us and we couldn't understand their local dialect. Otherwise, there were the odd little scraps. I remember one boy having a go at my brother Sid and I had to step in.

'We always went to Evensong, then all walk home together, led by Lady Constance and Lady Audrey.

'One time, Eddie Jennings, who lived back on Knowle Lane, had a pack of cigarettes. Each boy took a puff. We got home and the old man called us over. "A little birdie tells me you two have been smoking. I hope I never find out you smoke."

'Jimmy Jeffreys lost an eye in the First World War. He was a robust fellow and when you went into his store, you never knew if he'd be grouchy or kind.

'Loveridge's at the bottom of Church Street was where we bought food. Iris (Ernie's sister) worked for them for a while. I would drop the ration books off with Mrs Loveridge. She would fill orders, clip out all the bits from books, and Mr L would deliver it out to Knowle the next day.

'Whilst staying at Knowle House, during the summer school holidays, the children were sent for a break. One year, my brother and me were sent to Simonsbath where we stayed with a Mrs Purchase and her son, Danny.

'Another year, we went to Exford. We stayed with a Mrs Slocum, who lived in a house at the kennels of the Somerset staghounds. Her husband would have been employed there, but we never saw him. He could well have been called up, the same with Mr Purchase. It was interesting at Simonsbath, as 'peat' was being used as fuel. And we had a go at "churning" butter, which was quite hard work.

'At Exford, we could watch the hounds being fed. They were let out into the field to feed on carcasses, watched over and controlled by some of the hunt staff.

'Bath night at Knowle was of a Friday night. My granddaughter was aghast to think that we only bathed once a week. We were sent to the bathroom, bathed under supervision, and given a cup of senna pod tea to drink that was drunk as quickly as possible (It was to keep us regular).'

Maurice Huxtable

'At that time, the Munsons were living in the stable at Knowle. Two separate buildings, one on each side. They were living on one side, and another family on the other side. There was a fire in there and burned a lot down. Stenner had to go down and shoot one bull because it was upset and they couldn't take him out. They took out a couple, but this one was too riled up. Stenner was a butcher at Williton – Sammy he was called – the son of our butcher here.

'I was 16, 17, and it was a Friday night and we were practicing cricket down there on the cricket field when it happened. The field belonged to Lady Audrey and Lady Ryder. There used to be two horses there. We had to get them out before we could practise.'

Chas Mehegan

'As four young boys, we were always out together, up to all sorts of mischief. We would go for long walks, sometimes out all day. On one occasion, we walked to Dunkery Beacon on Exmoor, and during a storm we all tried to shelter under a small tree. I remember my brother Jimmy being frightened by the *thunder and lightning. On the way back, we came across an old farm where they made cider. We tried eating some apples we found, but they were too sour.*

'On one occasion during the school holidays, we all went to Minehead by the local bus, which was a lovely old Bedford. I've always remembered the whining sound the engine made going up hills. Minehead had a lovely sandy beach, which was destroyed in a storm some years later.

'Some distance from the village was a big country house where there was a Rookery. I remember climbing up the trees to get some eggs to take home to cook. In the autumn, the men had a Rook shoot, which we as children thought exciting. Today it would be illegal.

'I was once dared by the others to climb up to a buzzard hawk's nest, which I did. The birds attacked me and I beat a hasty retreat. I fell the last 10 or 15 feet.'

Brian Lambert

'We would go up on the moors to pick whortleberries, which would be used for colouring jams and dye for uniforms. We would get paid 6p a basket.

'At weekends, we would walk over the moors to Minehead. We'd sit on any part of the beach, which was open to the public. On the rare occasion, we went to the cinema.

'I can't remember much about school until we went back to London. To get to school in Timberscombe, we walked from Knowle, past a garage. School was east of the church. There was a blacksmith – Coles – and I remember watching him shoe horses. It was a burnt pungent smell, burning a shoe into place and chopping off toe nails.

'The corner of Brook Street was tight. RAF transported parts of planes and a wing got stuck on the sharp left turn around one cottage. It was coming from Minehead, going into the village, where the stone wall runs along the stream.'

★ ★ ★

Exmoor made two special contributions to the country during the war – rabbits and herbs. Rabbit catching intensified after 1939, and the Barnstable-Taunton branch of the GWR had a 'rabbit train' at full load every night – 16,000 rabbits. Usually, some 2,400 carcasses were picked up at Dulverton Station.

Wild plants were gathered for medicinal purposes by repeating the 1914-1918 supply of sphagnum moss for wound pads. Imported drug plants ceased, and now the Ministry of Supply had to appeal for foxglove leaf and seed, belladonna, henbane, nettle leaves, sphagnum moss and rose hips. Foxglove leaf and seed were the most important because of their value as heart medicine and became the nation's sole source of digitalis. Leaves were taken to drying stations in Allerford, Exford, Wiveliscombe and Dulverton.

Several evacuees remember an elderly bearded man whose artist's studio was down the hill from Holes Square. In 1939, John Arthur Mease Lomas, in his late 70s, lived at Owey Viene in Cowbridge. His wife, Mary Christine, also an artist, art critic and an enameller, had died the previous December.

After formal training in Europe, Lomas had returned to Minehead, where his family lived and he worked to develop his unique painting style. He was a perfectionist and half-finished canvases were stacked around the walls in his studio.

By chance, in April 1906, a financier from London on holiday discovered his work and persuaded the artist to let him arrange an exhibition in London. Lomas's powerful depictions of the West Somerset landscape were met with great enthusiasm by the London art world. Critics said he was one of the most brilliant and original landscape painters of the day. In the 1920s, he and Mary left the whirlwind of London and moved back to Somerset, where he worked alone, isolated in this remote country village for the rest of his life.

Ernie Munson

'As for Mr Lomas, the artist, I can remember him as an old grey-haired gentleman with a grey beard. He appeared to keep very much to himself. His dwelling was very much in the style of a chalet, built on stilts. There

was a flight of stairs to get to his front door. As it was built for him by Frank Huxtable on a slope, the front was supported by wooden pillars. It was in the field where the current row of houses is, which I believe is called Willow Bank.'

Thomas Robinson

'We got on quite well with locals. Most evacuees in the village were with good families. Some complained about where they were living and they didn't stay too long. If they weren't treated well, or if they weren't being looked after, they just went home or their parents would come get them.'

* * *

In 1945, threats of V2 long-range rocket bombardment continued in London. When the war ended in Europe, special trains went into service to take evacuees home though the majority had already found their way back. Those still in the Exmoor area came nowhere near to filling the trains.

Many evacuees could not return to the city because their homes no longer existed. Local housing authorities in Somerset had to assume responsibility for finding them places to live. Their residence in the countryside, which had been meant to be temporary, now seemed permanent.

10

Billy Lambert

Brian Lambert

'The scooter was Billy's, and he loved it. I did, too, and when he was at school, I got to play on it. We went to pick him up at school that day and Billy took over the scooter. We were on our way to see the Gandes – one boy and two girls. Eddie, the boy, was younger than me.

'My brother was on his scooter in front of us in the narrow country lane behind Knowle. My mother was pushing me in a pushchair and coming toward us was a coal lorry – one of the very few vehicles during the war that could use petrol.

'Our mother pushed the pram into the entryway to let it pass. The driver saw us, but not Billy. My brother could see the lorry, so he pushed into the field gate on the left. The lorry pulled into the gate to let us pass and hit my brother. He died at the scene. It was May 10, 1941.

'Father came out from London when Billy was killed.'

Eddie Gande

'Mrs Lambert was pushing the pram down the road with Brian in it, Jean beside her, and Billy was on his scooter. It was a long, narrow road. Billy backed into the gate to make room for a coal lorry. The lorry driver went into reverse to give Mrs Lambert room to pass and that's when he ran over Billy, who was standing by the gateway. Jean came running back to us saying Billy had been killed. My mother went back to be with Mrs Lambert until the ambulance came.'

Above: Billy Lambert (1933–1941)
(courtesy of David Lambert)

Brian Lambert

'*My mum saw the lorry try to miss her and realised that it had pulled into the gate where Billy was. After he was killed, it was never the same. Being there in a strange place and losing him was extremely difficult for her.*'

Roy Smith

'*While we were there, one boy was killed. He had come from Lambeth and I can't remember his name, but he had been evacuated along with his mother, and they were living behind the house in some flats above the stables. Knowle was a massive big place, with flats and cottages all around the house for the staff, the maintenance men, the herdsmen, the groom, the gamekeepers.*

'*This boy got crushed when a dung lorry backed up against a wall. He was killed instantly, and all the Cubs, Boy Scouts, Brownies and Girl Guides went to the funeral with Lady Audrey and Lady Constance. This was the Timberscombe Parish church, and everyone was there for the service. His coffin was so little, and afterwards they carried him out to the graveyard and put him down the hole, and we all walked past the open grave and gave him our salutes. I don't think most of them knew what to say, but my parents had taught me. "Rest in Peace," I said.'*

Brian Lambert

'Joyce Robinson saw Billy being killed. She was just a girl. She was out that day with some others, collecting metal (cast iron) for the war effort. Years ago, I left a note for her in the church book and sometime later, she got in touch with me. I don't remember that we talked about Billy.'

Ernie Munson

'Not that long ago, I visited the church, and the whole graveyard was tended, it seemed like, except for Billy Lambert's grave.

'Imagine, get evacuated from London, come down to Somerset, and get killed by a lorry.'

Brian Lambert

'The government moved us out to the countryside to protect us, but if we had stayed in London, Billy would have survived. Our house on Autumn Street wasn't hit by German bombs.

'When you're a kid, you don't understand death. You always expect he'll come back. Jean maintained a memory of Billy her entire life.'

Above: Billy Lambert's grave in Timberscombe churchyard

11

The Night the German Bomber Crashed

Every conversation with these evacuees moves toward two significant memories: the death of Billy Lambert and the night a Junkers Ju 88 twin-engine Schnellbomber crashed just outside the village.

Maurice Huxtable

'I remember a plane coming across here all afire, must have been about 3:00 in the night, and my mother woke me up. My father was away in the army. She called me in her bedroom, and we looked out the window. This plane came straight across here, all afire. And then landed up Boehm. By the time we got up there, there were police up there and it was all cordoned off. There was one that bailed out. Landed by parachute at Luxborough. And there was this man going to work and this chap, this German, wanted to give himself up and the man said: 'I haven't got time now, I'm already late for work.' There was four in the plane. One man came down somewhere else, and the other two were killed. Apparently, they'd been bombing in Cardiff.

'Another time, there was a plane that went down at Grabbist. That was during the day. That one came down and crashed on Porlock Beach.'

Ernie Munson

'I was living at Knowle at the time. The noise woke me up. It sounded like the plane flew overhead. I tried to get a good look at the wreckage, but of course, the law kept us well away. I can picture the crash site now. It was in the field of the willow plantation.

'I can also remember the smell. This may sound strange, but years ago, I bought a telescope for bird watching. It is of a German make and encased in a kind of rubberised compound. The smell of that compound is exactly the smell I experienced at the crash site, and it still reminds me of it.'

Thomas Robinson

Tom Robinson was living at Knowle, in the big house, at the time of the crash and remembers hearing the plane go down in flames. He says they could smell burning flesh.

'Another time, during the day, there was a plane noise with a rat-a-tat-tat of machine gun fire overhead. We were in school. It seemed funny that most of us Londoners ran to the windows to see a Spitfire chasing a German bomber which unloaded a bomb on Dunkery Beacon but was shot down. The local children dived under the desks as they had probably practiced.'

Patricia Herniman

In her memoir, Pat Herniman wrote that her Aunt Kath recalled a scary experience in the 'Battle of Britain'. Her version was that 'a crippled German bomber flew low over the mill where she was living and along the Avill Valley in an endeavour to find a landing area, probably having been damaged by the guns sited on the Brendon hills. She watched from her bedroom window as the plane crash-landed. Three crew members bailed out and walked down into the village to surrender; the remaining two, the pilot and navigator, were found by villagers who discovered one of them literally hung by the neck.

Once the excitement died down, Maurice Huxtable snuck over to Boehm Farm and clipped off a square metal piece of the plane – a treasure he kept all these years in a small plastic bag. He's looked for it so he could show it to us, but he has never found it.

★ ★ ★

After Germany opened the blitz in the autumn of 1940, there were nights when people heard raiders on their way to bomb industrial and military objectives on the other side of the Bristol Channel. The raiders' flight path took them over Exmoor and West Somerset and that produced the bombing occurrences, the load-shedding.

Jack Hurley related the crash incident in his book, *Exmoor in Wartime 1939-1945* (The Exmoor Press, 1978).

> An enemy airman's silent descent from the skies.... But he would not be the kind of parachutist for whom we had scanned the skies in 1940. Now, in 1943, he would be no more than a 'baler' from a doomed plane. So it was in the small hours of May 18th, when Otto Bok and Albert Wurtz parted with their crashing Junkers and floated down in the moonlight towards fields near Luxborough.
>
> The plane was returning from a raid on Cardiff when it was intercepted and damaged by one of our night fighters. North of the Brendon Hills, the enemy's doom was near. The plane missed the buildings at Beasley Farm, Timberscombe, and a few on toward the village before crashing into a willow tree plantation at Boehm and catching fire. Three airmen perished. The crash into the trees averted a tragedy right in Timberscombe village, about 500 yards away.
>
> Meanwhile, Otto Bok and Albert Wurtz (the latter was the wireless operator) had landed near Stowey, between Roadwater and Luxborough. The time of the incident 3:15 had been fixed by Bok himself. Years after the war, in a letter to Clifford Vincent, of Bristol, who has compiled records of enemy airmen landings on English soil, Bok said he remembered looking at his watch as he completed his fall.
>
> Now, 20 years later, interested in learning where he and Wurtz had come down, he could supply a few details about the terrain he had glimpsed in the half-light. He also

mentioned that he saw two men climb a hedge into a field.

Clifford Vincent wrote to the *West Somerset Press*, passing on the details Bok had given, and there was a prompt response. Among those who were about in the area that May night were Walter and Claude Case and Cyril Burge. The last-named, who was working on a farm at Rodhuish during the war, has recalled seeing the damaged plane in its last minutes of light, and says he went on a search with Claude Case, the latter having glimpsed an airman bailing out. Also, a pistol shot had been heard. It could have been a signal to an airman colleague.

The searchers did not find the airmen, but they came upon a parachute folded up in a wheat field. They decided the airman must have gone in the Luxborough direction to find his mate, and as they continued their search, they found the plane's gun turret and guns in a field on Styles farm, Rodhuish, about two miles from Luxborough.

In his letter to Clifford Vincent, Otto Bok said he was taken prisoner by two 'middle-aged soldiers', one of whom was Kenneth Grabham of Timberscombe.

Whatever happened, Bok and his comrade were not long at large. Bok, taken to Minehead police station, found Wurtz waiting to greet him. It was in this incident that an imperishable anecdote had its root. Both Cyril Burge and Kenneth Grabham have mentioned it. One airman tried to give himself up to a farm worker he met at dawn, and who reacted with these immortal words: 'No, I can't be bothered with'ee. I be late for work as 'tis!

Maurice Huxtable

'I've got a write up, which is all wrong. Some people say—There were all sorts of stories of what people saw, but they never did. It came across here. I know what happened because I saw it.'

12

Norman Sutton Joins the Slade Family Orchestra

Herbie Slade's band was a regular feature at weekend dances around Exmoor. Herbie played the squeeze box and his 14-year-old-son Roy played the piano accordion, and sometimes the drums. Soon Herbie recruited Norman Sutton into the band.

Norman played the bass drum and kettle drum with brushes, and Roy stayed on the piano accordion. Norman was keen to be a part of the orchestra, and Herbie paid him a tenner once or twice for his time.

Herbie would take his motorcycle with a sidecar from his garage and the family would go down country lanes on a late weekend afternoon. Norman and Elizabeth would ride in the sidecar, along with the musical instruments, and they would go play for dances either in Timberscombe, Wheddon Cross, Luccombe, Wootten Courtenay, or other nearby villages.

Wherever they went, the dances were always popular because it gave people an evening when they could forget the war. Village girls would chat up British soldiers who were camped nearby. At one dance, a soldier came up to Norman and said: 'You come from Canning Town, don't you? I live just down the road from you.' Norman was caught off-guard. Here he was, in a village hall in Exmoor, reminded of home all at once. This young soldier knew him in that other world, one so different from where he was living at the moment.

Norman remembers they played music of the day, couples dancing the Foxtrot and the quickstep. Two or three couples in a line, arm in arm, would dance the uniform steps of the Palais Glide to "Horsey, Horsey". The dance was sweeping the country.

The Slades' performances were strictly instrumental, though as the evening wore on, others would sing. One night, Norman got the idea that he wanted to sing, too. He stood up behind the drums and sang "My Grandfather's Clock", which was a standard of British brass and colliery bands, accompanied by Herbie and Roy. He sang more often at dances after that, often including an upbeat version of the popular tune "Little Sir Echo."

'Little sir echo - how do you do? Hel... lo,'

Herbie, Elizabeth, and Roy would join in on the echo: *'Hel... lo'*

'Won't you come over and play?'

'... and play'

At first, only the Slades sang the echo parts of the lyrics, but soon everyone in the hall would join in - *hello* or *play* or *away*.

Here people knew him, knew he could do things. They treated him like one of their own rather than just an East End street urchin from Canning Town.

13

Going Back

Then it was over.

The Union Jack was run-up on Dunkery Beacon. On VE and VJ day, street parties crowded the High Street in Dunster and stretched up to the Luttrell's lawn. Mrs Willis closed the school for two days of celebration. Within a short time, several industrious mothers ripped down blackout material and made uniforms out of them for the boys on the football team.

John Gratton

'When the Russians moved westward, the Germans abandoned Auschwitz, the POW camp in Poland where my father was held, and marched the prisoners westward. About a six-hundred-mile march, about twenty miles a day, before they caught up with the Americans. They met them in mid Germany. They'd been POWs for so long.

'My mother had News of the World maps on her bedroom walls. The Red Cross would deliver them. She had been able to tell where my father was in Europe. It kept her going that he was still alive.

'I was five and a half or six when he was liberated. We were at Dunster at the time. We were on a coach going to Minehead. My grandfather stopped the coach at Parham's Corner, running up to say there was a telegram that he had been liberated. The coach was elated because everyone knew everyone else.

'He knocked on our door. A neighbour had found him down at the railway station, unable to carry his kit back up because he was weak. My mother was overjoyed at seeing him.

Above: John Gratton and parents, Maurice and Phyllis Gratton (1946)
(courtesy of John Gratton)

'He was quite ill when he came home. Then he had to go back to the barracks in Deal. We went with him. Lodged at a farmhouse in Folkestone. Lodged for a few months. When we came back out to the council house in [Dunster] Marsh, his nerves were quite bad. He was a gardener before he went into the Marines, and he went back to gardening. Most of the old forces officers would give him work. They looked out for him.

'When he came home, he was very family orientated. We built a pig sty. He made cricket bats for all of us kids in the road. He cycled from Marsh to Withycombe to get me fireworks for firework night. He bought them from Stevens in Withycombe.'

Thomas Robinson

Tom had lived at Knowle since he was 10. At 14, the war was still going on, and he returned to London and worked as an office boy on the docks.

'At 15, I became an apprentice carpenter and joiner, a five-year apprenticeship where they were building Mulberry Harbours, ready for the D-Day invasion of France.

'I came back west for a holiday a few years later. Lady Ryder had died, but Lady Audrey was still there. I stayed with the Yeandles that trip, the big house on the left, across from the mill on the Old Dunster Road, headed into Timberscombe village.'

Roy Smith

'My mother inherited a house at 301 Sterne Road, Manor Park, East Ham, from my Auntie Nell, which meant that Mum and Dad could move away from the docks and take us all back to London, although I was still sent back to Somerset a few months later to go to an approved school over that business with the boy and the window cord.

'The approved school was at Blue Anchor, and during that time I got my first job in panto, playing Bonzo the dog in a Richmond Theatre production of Babes in the Woods.

'Somerset kept calling me back. In the cold winter of 1947, I went back for 16 or 17 weeks. Came to Timberscombe first because I was getting a few quid, this way and that, doing naughty things, and could stay in the country pubs. From there I went on to Wootton Courtenay, Dunster, Alcombe and Minehead, where I went back to see the nurses who had looked after me when I had my operations.

'In summers, the family would go out in caravans. Mum and Dad in the caravan and the boys in one trailer, the girls in another. The first summer, we went down to Somerset. Timberscombe had upset me because Lady Constance and Lady Audrey were dead and Knowle seemed dilapidated after the war.

'The land and the farm seemed poorer. Behind the house, they used to have an aviary with what I called Puss-in-Boots bantams. Those black and *white birds with the frills around their feet, that had all gone and so had the breeding pheasants, the ponies and the shire horses. The stables seemed bare. They were quiet and empty. And the house didn't seem the same anymore.'*

In a 1999 *Guardian* article, Tory London mayoral candidate, Andrew Boff admitted his uncle, Roy "Little Legs" Smith, was a "midget mafia" wrestler at a Soho club and had played a Dalek in *Doctor Who*. Smith claimed to have had 22 criminal convictions, including one for shooting a man in a London club. The 4ft 2 bit-part actor appeared in the Beatles' *Magical Mystery Tour* film and in several pantomimes as one of Snow White's little helpers. Mr Boff, however, insisted that claims by his mother's brother that he performed "smacky-bum jobs" for east London gangsters Ron and Reggie Kray were idle boasts.

In his memoir, Roy bragged that he knew John Wayne, Elizabeth Taylor and Paul McCartney and claimed that Marlon Brando asked him to join the cast of *The Wild One*.

According to the *Guardian* article, Roy told how, despite being only 50 inches tall, he knee-capped people who upset him with an iron bar and slashed their bottoms because he could not reach their faces. Knocking back two bottles of whisky a day before he died, Roy was well-known to theatre and cinema goers who saw him busking outside the Odeon in the West End's Leicester Square.

Ronald "Ronnie" Kray and Reginald "Reggie" Kray, twin brothers, were the foremost perpetrators of organised crime in the East End of London, involved in murder, armed robbery, arson and protection rackets. They were once called the most evil men in Britain. Charlie Kray, Ronnie and Reggie's elder brother, once said about Roy: 'It's the biggest load of rubbish I've heard. I only met him once. All I know about him was that he had blocks fitted on the car pedals so that he could reach the brakes.'

Norman Sutton

Norman, the last surviving of the Sutton brothers, returned to London with a Somerset accent after the war. Years after their return, when they were grown, Jack, Adrian and he went back to Timberscombe for a visit. Some places they remembered were gone, like the Bryan's house, where Adrian and Peter had lived. Almost all the village looked the same, but it wasn't. Mrs Willis was gone. Another headmistress was in her place, teaching children unfamiliar to them. Huxtables still lived where they had always lived, but it was no longer a petrol station. Jeffrey's store was now the village post office, and Ye Olde Malt House, once the butcher 's shop, had been converted into a dwelling, and Maurice Huxtable, who they knew as a boy, was living there with his family. New people tended to their daily affairs as though the cottages and the pub and the village had always belonged to them.

Jackie Gande Nunney
After the war, the Gandes went back to London. Louisa's husband, Frederick, worked as a painter/decorator for the National Trust, and Louisa kept in touch with the Trust in Somerset. Finally, she was told that a cottage and a job for Frederick as a painter at a Trust property was available in the vale between Tivington and Porlock – Paradise Valley. Eventually, they would settle in Luccombe.

Eddie Gande
In London, Eddie went to Poplar Tech to become an electrician. He was eager to return to Somerset with the family so he could work on a farm again, which he did for two and a half years. After a three-year stint in the army, he worked at a saw mill in Slough and then a cable factory. Then he came back to Somerset, to Luccombe, and worked as a cable jointer, laying underground cables.

Ernie Munson
The last day in London, the day they were evacuated, is imprinted on his memory. Mums and dads on pavements, waving as they walked past, boarding the train.

Above: Scouts at Dunster Beach (1945)
Ernie Munson (in front), Sid Munson (facing camera)
(courtesy of Ernie Munson)

In the beginning, Grace and Iris were like a lot of children who went back to London after a few months. They returned to Timberscombe when the bombing started in May 1940.

At 14, Ernie left school and went to work with his father and Frank Huxtable at Dunster beach. They built huts that were occupied by the American army during the war. At 15, he joined the Royal Navy.

When they left Knowle, the Munson family moved to a council house in Dunster. Ernie lost contact with the boys from the village. From then on, until Sid's death in 2014, he and his brother never spoke of their short time living with the Veales or Chatworthys without their parents. They kept their feelings about being together as evacuees to themselves.

Brian Lambert

'Nothing was the same after Billy died.

'The ladies wanted us to pay rent at Knowle and it was too much, so we moved back to London. My dad couldn't afford to keep two households, one in London, which was 15s 6p a week, and the other in Timberscombe at Knowle. We returned to London at the beginning of 1943, just in time for the V1 and V2 rocket attacks. I went to school at Attley Road School.

'Eddie Gande came back to Autumn Street after the war, too. We would play together in the park, like we used to before we all went away.

'During the war, cast-iron railings all over the East End were removed and replaced with wood fences. They said the iron was needed for the war effort. When they didn't use any of it, we found out later, they threw all of it in the Irish Sea. The cast-iron railings in Mayfair were left in place as they'd always been.

'The past is tinged with the way you felt at the time. In East London, people were kept in ignorance by that Victorian attitude: don't educate them and they will do as they're told.

'My parents left and moved to Slough when the East End of London was cleared of 'slum dwellings.' The government forgot to tell us that the houses we lived in for many years were slums. We never knew how others lived. We all thought that everyone lived like we did. Two rooms up, two rooms down, a kitchen, a tin bath hanging on the back wall and an outside toilet. The house was always clean, and most of the time warm, when we could get coal and the miners were not on strike. There was always enough food. We lived in a home, not a slum. We accepted how we lived.'

John Gratton

'Joycie Thurtle left school at fourteen and went to work in Floyd's Department Store in Minehead. It took up Mother's coupon allowance to get her work clothes. She stayed until my father came home and then came back to have her holidays with us. Even when she was married, even right until she died, she was with us all the time.

'A lot of the evacuees stayed. Boosted village populations. Poor little kids trailing behind a vicar they had never known because they had been put on a train in London and suddenly were in Dunster or another rural place.

'Children torn away from parents and trusted to someone strange to bring them up. It was an experience that will never happen again.'

Brian Lambert

'I often think about everyone who's buried in that churchyard at St Petrock's. Who remembers them? Some have been buried there since the 1700s. Some were only buried five to six years ago. Grass grows and no one remembers. The last time I was there, I could still make out Billy's name on his stone. It hasn't worn away:William Lambert. He's next to the walkway that goes around the church. Someone's planted daffodils beside him.'

Beginning in 1939, official and unofficial evacuees would call this village home for as short as a week and some up to five years. In all, there were 175 of them. When I found current addresses for most of them, letters were either not returned or when they were, they had hand-written notes on the front, like "The lady has died." Most sons and daughters of the evacuees told me that their parent rarely had a word to say about the years of their childhood in Timberscombe.

For some children, the joy of coming home became a struggle after being away for so long, after the distress of evacuation.

For them, the war did not end in 1945.

Timberscombe School Evacuees – Children and Mothers (1939-1952): From School Admission Register

Jeanne Robinson: *Born*: 6-28-29; *Admission*: 11-9-39; *Parents*: Frank; *Address*: Kiln House c/o Prole; *Last school*: Havering Rd. Romford, Essex; *Last attendance*: 21-2-40; *Cause of leaving*: Returned to London.

Patricia M Robinson: *Born:* 9-9-31; *Admission:* 11-9-39; *Parents:* Frank; *Address:* Kiln House c/o Prole; *Last school:* Havering Rd. Romford, Essex; *Last attendance:* 21-2-40; *Cause of leaving:* Returned to London.

Sidney Munson: *Born:* 11-2-34; *Admission:* 1-9-39; *Parents:* George and Dora; *Address:* (1) Hill View c/o Thos. and Frances Veale (2) Knowle c/o Lady Ryder.

Ernest W Munson: *Born:* 30-9-31; *Admission:* 11-9-39; *Parents*: George and Dora; Address: (1) Hill View c/o Thos. and Frances Veale (2) Ernest and Rosina Clatworthy, Great House Street (3) Knowle c/o Lady Ryder.

Iris EB Munson: *Born:* 2-2-29; *Admission:* 11-9-39; *Parents:* George and Dora; *Address:* (1) 1 Council House c/o Robert and Blanche Baker (2) Knowle c/o Lady Ryder.

Grace Munson: *Born:* 30-5-27; *Admission:* 11-9-39; *Address:* (1) 1 Council House c/o Robert and Blanche Baker (2) Knowle c/o Lady Ryder.

John S Denwood: *Born:* 23-6-32; *Admission:* 11-9-39; *Address:* Knowle c/o Mrs. Bowles; *Cause for leaving:* Removed to Cambridge.

David Harnwell: *Born:* 31-5-33; *Admission:* 11-9-39; *Cause for leaving*: Removed to Luccombe, 5-4-40.

James Robinson: *Born:* 1-4-34; *Admission:* 11-9-39; *Address:* Knowle c/o Lady Ryder; *Home address:* West Ham, Essex.

William Lambert: *Born:* 13-3-33; *Admission:* 11-9-39; *Parents:* William and Elizabeth; *Address:* The Stables, Knowle; *Home address:* 14 Autumn Street, Bow E3; Accidently killed by a lorry.

Jean Lambert: *Born:* 9-1-35; *Admission:* 11-9-39; *Parents:* William and Elizabeth; *Address:* The Stables, Knowle; *Home address:* 14 Autumn Street, Bow E3; *Cause for leaving:* Return to London, 1943.

Brian Lambert: *Born:* 4-1-37; *Admission:* 15-9-41; *Parents:* William and Elizabeth; *Address:* The Stables, Knowle; *Home address:* 14 Autumn Street, Bow E3; *Cause for leaving:* Return to London, 1943.

Elizabeth Sinfield Lambert: *Born:* 1908; *Address:* The Stables, Knowle; *Occupation;* listed as unpaid domestic help at Knowle; *Home address:* 14 Autumn Street, Bow E3.

Derek Farmer: *Born:* 2-9-33; *Admission:* 18-9-39; *Parent:* Alfred; *Address:* Forge Cottages c/o Mrs Margaret Dyer; *Cause of leaving:* Returned to London, 21-2-40; *Home address:* Bromley Rd, Beckenham.

Eunice B Talbot: *Born:* 26-4-27; *Admission:* 11-9-39; *Address:* Coombe House c/o Mrs. Emily Eliza Coles; *Home address:* West Ham, Essex.

Evelyn May Talbot: *Born:* 30-1-32; *Admission:* 11-9-39; *Address:* Sunnyside c/o Thomas and Maud Brewer; *Home address:* West Ham, Essex.

Margaret P Talbot: *Born:* 14-8-30; *Admission:* 11-9-39; *Address:* Sunnyside c/o Thomas and Maud Brewer; *Home address:* West Ham, Essex.

Jean Burt: *Born*: 2-5-31; *Admission:* 20-9-39; *Parent*: George; *Address*: The Square c/o Mrs. J Baker; *Last school:* Grange Park Junior School, Hayes; *Cause for leaving*: Returned to London, 20-3-40.

Rosamond A. Cleverley: *Born*: 15-12-31; *Admission:* 25-9-39; *Parent*: Dorothy; *Address*: Bickham Manor; *Last school*: Horsendon Lane Juniors, Greenford; *Cause for leaving*: Returned to London, 20-10-39.

Dorothy Cleverley: *Born*: 07-03-1904; Rosamond's mother *Occupation:* Cook, Bickham Manor.

Brenda Simpkin: *Born*: 23-2-30; *Admission:* 25-9-39; *Parent*: Ethel; *Address*: P.O. Bungalow; *Last school*: Stag Lane Junior; *Cause for leaving:* Returned to London, 10-29-39.

Frank Simpkin: *Born*: 29-3-27; *Admission:* 9-10-39; *Parent*: Ethel; *Address*: P.O. Bungalow; *Last school:* Stag Lane Junior ; *Cause for leaving*: Returned to London, 20-10-39.

David Munson: *Born*: 7-1941; *Parents*: George and Dora; *Address*: Knowle Manor; Died: 7-1941. Survived 4 days.

John Munson: *Born*: 18-12-1944; *Parents*: George and Dora Munson; *Address*: Knowle Manor.

Anna J Sparkes: *Born*: 4-3-26; *Address*: Rosslyn c/o Mrs. Grace Yeandle; *Home address:* West Ham, Essex.

Ena D. Roach: *Born*: 23-3-26; *Address*: Rosslyn c/o Mrs. Grace Yeandle; *Home Address:* West Ham, Essex.

Ronald Leslie Dedman: *Born*: 15-10-25; *Address*: 3 Council Cottage c/o Grace Huxtable; *Home address:* West Ham, Essex.

Iris A.A. Oliver: *Born*: 29-10-26; *Address*: The Gardens c/o Bessie Clatworthy; *Home address:* Romford, Essex.

Doreen Louise Gibbs: *Born*: 3-8-33; Address: The Old Mill c/o Mrs Ray; *Home address:* West Ham, Essex.

Arthur Oliver: *Born*: 30-10-28; *Address*: c/o Henry Cane and Adam Maud Cane; *Home address:* West Ham, Essex.

Frederick J. Wells: **Born:** 4-26; *Address:* Ford Cottage c/o Ernest and Eliza Ferris; *Home address:* West Ham, Essex.

Frederick J Elton: *Born*: 4-4-26; *Address*: Ford Cottage c/o George and Evelyn May Elford. Brother of John P Elton.

Elsie EJ Lawrence: *Born*: 24-5-27; *Address*: Berrowcote c/o Frederick and Elsie Norman.

Edna VF Smith: *Born*: 24-6-27; *Address*: Berrowcote c/o Frederick and Elsie Norman.

Alvis Neville Carter: *Born*: 20-2-28; *Address*: Kiln Farm c/o Prole; *Home address:* Wayside, Grays, Essex.

Maud Carter: *Born*: 16-2-94; *Occupation*: unpaid domestic duties; *Home address*: Wayside, Grays, Essex. Mother of Alvis Carter.

John Lancelot Blades Percival: *Born*: 26-7-33; *Address*: Rosemount Cottage; *Cause for leaving*: Entered Sherborne School, Dorset.

Beryl Pike: *Born:* 5-31; *Home address*: Bristol.

John P. Elton: *Born:* 1-31; *Home address:* West Ham, Canning Town, Essex. Brother of Frederick J Elton.

Shirley Burt: *Born:* 19-1-35; *Admission:* 8-1-40; *Parent:* George; *Address:* The Square c/o Mrs. J Baker; *Cause for leaving*: Returned to London, 20-3-40.

George Hadlow: *Born*: 31-3-33; *Admission*: 12-2-40; *Parents*: Fred and Ada; *Address*: 6 Council Houses c/o Ivan and Charlotte R Bircham; *Home address*: Castle Street, East Ham; *Cause for leaving*: Returned to London.

Jean Hadlow: *Born:* 15-6-35; *Admission:* 17-6-40; *Parents*: Fred and Anna; *Address*: 6 Council Houses c/o Ivan Bircham; *Cause for leaving:* Returned home.

William Robinson: *Born*: 30-7-31; *Admission*: 11-9-39; *Address*: Knowle c/o Lady Ryder; *Home address*: West Ham, Essex.

Robert Ernest Robinson: Born: 22-11-25; *Admission*: 11-9-39; *Address*: Knowle c/o Lady Ryder; *Home address:* West Ham, Essex.

Thomas Robinson: *Born*: 15-10-29; *Admission*: 11-9-39; *Address*: Knowle c/o Lady Ryder; *Home address*: West Ham, Essex.

Joyce Robinson: *Born*: 27-11-27; *Admission*: 11-9-39; *Address*: Knowle c/o Lady Ryder; *Home address*: West Ham, Essex.

Peter Wallace Sutton: *Born*: 2-12-26; *Admission*: 11-9-39; *Address*: Brook House c/o Alfred Bryan; *Home address*: Canning Town, Essex.

John (Jack) Sutton: *Born*: 6-10-27; *Admission*: 11-9-39; *Address*: 28 Cendle Terrace, The Square c/o Ferris; *Home address:* Canning Town, Essex.

Adrian Paul Sutton: *Born:* 14-5-32; *Admission*: 11-9-39; *Address*: Brook House c/o Alfred Bryan; *Home address*: Canning Town, Essex.

Norman Sutton: *Born:* 11-9-39; *Admission*: 04-30; *Address*: Holes, The Square c/o Herbert Slade; *Home Address:* Canning Town, Essex.

Raymond Smith: *Born:* 16-12-33; *Admission*: 11-9-39; *Address*: Knowle c/o Lady Ryder; *Home address:* West Ham, Essex.

Royston Smith: *Born*: 30-20-31; *Admission*: 11-9-39; *Address*: Knowle c/o Lady Ryder; *Home address:* West Ham, Essex.

Iris Smith: *Born*: 9-10-26; *Admission*: 11-9-39; *Address*: Knowle c/o Lady Ryder; *Home address*: West Ham, Essex.

Mary E Smith: *Born*: 2-4-29; Admission: 11-9-39; *Address*: Knowle c/o Lady Ryder; *Home address*: West Ham, Essex.

Louisa Gande: *Born*: 18-12-11; *Address*: (1) The Stables, Knowle (2) The Bungalow, Knowle Lane (3) Croydon Farm (4) Luccombe; *Home address:* 17, Autumn Street, Bow E3.

Maureen Gande: *Born*: 24-4-35; *Admission*: 11-9-39; *Parents*: Louisa and Fred; *Address*: (1) The Stables, Knowle (2) The Bungalow, Knowle Lane (3) Croydon Farm (4) Luccombe; *Home address:* 17, Autumn Street, Bow E3.

Edwin F Gande: *Born*: 12-11-36; *Admission*: 11-9-39; *Parents*: Louisa and Fred; *Address*: (1) The Stables, Knowle (2) The Bungalow, Knowle Lane (3) Croydon Farm (4) Luccombe; *Home address:* 17, Autumn Street, Bow E3.

Jacqueline Gande: *Born*: 10-41, Irnham Lodge, Minehead; Parents: Louisa and Fred; *Address*: (1) The Stables, Knowle (2) The Bungalow, Knowle Lane (3) Croydon Farm (4) Luccombe; *Home address:* 17, Autumn Street, Bow E3.

Patricia (Pamela) Gande: *Born*: 10-38; *Parents*: Louisa and Fred; *Address*: (1) The Stables, Knowle (2) The Bungalow, Knowle Lane (3) Croydon Farm (4) Luccombe; *Home address:* 17, Autumn Street, Bow E3.

Bernard Gande: *Born*: 9-4-33. *Admission*: 11-9-39; *Address*: The Gardens c/o Mrs. Webber; *Last School*: Gainsborough Road, Hackney; *Home address:* 7, Berkshire Road, Hackney. Cousin to Maureen, Eddie, Patricia and Jackie Gande.

Iris May Rose White: *Born*: 20-3-35; *Admission*: 11-9-39; *Address*: Knowle c/o Lady Ryder; *Cause for leaving:* Removed to Dagenham.

Dorothy L. White: *Born*: 3-23-27; *Admission*: 11-9-39; *Address*: Knowle c/o Lady Ryder; *Cause for leaving:* Removed to Dagenham.

Joan L White: *Born*: 2-9-30; *Admission*: 11-9-39; *Address*: Knowle c/o Lady Ryder; Cause for leaving: Removed to Dagenham.

Tony Armstrong: *Born*: 12-8-30; *Admission*: 10-6-40; *Parent:* Douglas; *Address*: Bickham Farm; *Last school:* Ardingly College, Sussex; *Cause for leaving*: Evacuated to Canada, 26-7-40.

Jean Armstrong: *Born*: 21-1-27; *Admission*: 10-6-40; *Parent:* Douglas; *Address*: Bickham Farm ; *Last school*: Convent of Our Lady of Sion, Worthing, Sussex; *Cause for leaving*: Removed to Private School, 26-7-40.

Thomas Mayne: *Born*: 28-2-28; *Admission*: 7-6-40; *Parent:* Thomas; *Address*: Kiln House: *Home address:* Bush Elms, Sen. Romford, Essex; *Cause for leaving*: Removed to "Pengrose" Meadow Grove, Watchet.

Alan Mayne: *Born:* 9-1-30; *Admission*: 17-6-40; *Parent:* Thomas; *Address*: Kiln House; *Last school:* Ransford Way Junior, Romford, Essex; *Cause for leaving*: Removed to "Pengrose" Meadow Grove, Watchet.

Joseph F. Farmer: *Born:* 23-8-39; *Admission*: 19-6-40; *Parent:* Chas.; *Address*: 3 Council Houses c/o Grace Huxtable; *Last school:* Hardly Sen. Southhampton; *Home address*: "Sunnyside" The Drove, Blackfield; *Cause for leaving*: Returned home.

Peter Bjook: *Born:* 31-8-34; *Admission*: 1-7-40; *Parent:* Lorna; *Address*: Knapp; *Home address:* Pope Street, Eltham, Kent; Cause for leaving: Returned to London, 4-7-40.

Lilian Colman: *Born*: 15-7-33; *Admission*: 30-8-39; *Parent:* David; *Address*: Church Steps; *Last school:* Llllanhilleth Junior; *Cause for leaving*: Returned to Sales.

Kenneth Henderson: *Born*: 18-5-30; *Admission*: 9-7-40; *Parent:* Ivan; *Home address*: 2, Ash Rod Causeway, Sandwich Kent.

Cyril Leatherby: *Born*: 28-1-27; *Admission*: 3-9-40; Parent: Ethel; *Address*: Church Steps; *Last school*:   Westover Senior, Bridgwater; Home address: 1 Penzoy Ave, Bridgwater.

Douglas Leatherby: *Born*: 10-11-30; *Admission*: 3-9-40; *Parent*: Ethel; *Address*: Church Steps; Last school: Eastover Junior; *Cause for leaving*: Left of age, 22-12-44.

Sadie Samson: *Born*: 4-7-36; *Admission*: 16-10-40; *Guardian*: Rev RAW Newman; *Address*: The Vicarage.

Eileen Gundry: *Born*: 25-1-27; *Admission*: 21-10-40; *Parent*: George; *Address*: c/o Mrs. F Bond P.O. Timberscombe; *Last school*: Crayford Central; *Home address:* 23, Wentworth Drive, Dartford, Kent; *Cause for leaving:* Returned home.

Sylvia James: *Born*: 11-5-34; *Admission*: 29-10-40; *Parent*: Ernest; *Address:* The Stores; *Last school:* Verondene Kindergarten School Park Ave.; *Cause for leaving*: Returned to London, 9-5-41.

Harry Dale: *Born*: 11-9-33; *Admission*: 6-11-40; *Parent:* Harry; *Address*: Knowle Manor c/oLady Ruder; *Home address*: 28 Royal Oak Road, Bexley Heath, Kent; Last school: *Upton Road School*; Cause for leaving: Returned to London.

Desmond Hutchings: *Born*: 22-10-35; *Admission*: 4-11-40; *Address*: Ford Cottage c/o Mrs. E Ferris (grandmother) Home address: 10, Boon's Place, Multey, Plymouth. *Date of return:* 13-8-44.

Anthony Hutchings: *Born*: 11-9-30; *Admission*: 6-1-36; *Address*: Ford Cottages c/o Mrs. E Ferris (grandmother); *Cause for leaving*: Of age, 26-10-44.

Stella Morris: *Born*: 10-5-33; *Admission*: 1-11-40; *Parent*: Beatrice; *Address*: Clouds, Wootten Courtenay; *Home address*: 38 Dryhill Rd. Belvedere; *Last school*: Kent Bedonwell Junior School.

June O. Perfect: *Born*: 7-6-34; *Admission*: 6-1-41; *Parent*: Amelia; *Address*: Croydon Farm; *Home address*: 19, Aperfield Rd Erith, Kent; *Last school*: Crescent Road School; *Cause for leaving:* Returned to Kent.

Peter A. Perfect: *Born*: 22-11-36; Admission: 6-1-41; *Parent*: Amelia; *Address*: Croydon Farm; *Last school:* Manor Road School; *Home address*: 19, Aperfield Rd Erith, Kent; *Cause for leaving*: Returned to Kent.

Michael Perfect: *Born*: 16-9-36; *Admission*: 1-12-41; *Parent*: Amelia; *Address*: Croydon Farm; *Home address*: 19, Aperfield Rd Erith, Kent.

Jean Gilbert: *Born*: 5-3-30; *Admission*: 6-1-41; *Parent*: Florence; *Address*: Croydon Farm; *Home address*: 29, Aperfield Rd. Erith, Kent; *Last school*: Manor Road School; *Cause for leaving*: Returned to Kent.

Alfred Gilbert: *Born:* 19-12-27; *Admission*: 6-1-41; *Parent*: Florence; *Address:* Croydon Farm; *Home address*: 29, Aperfield Rd, Erith, Kent; *Last school*: Manor Road School; *Cause for leaving*: Returned to Kent.

Joyce Gilbert: *Born*: 29-12-33; *Admission*: 6-1-41; *Parent*: Florence; *Address:* Croydon Farm; *Home address*: 29, Aperfield Rd, Erith Kent; *Last School*: Crescent Road School; *Cause for leaving:* Returned to Kent.

David Hopkins: *Born*: 2-12-34; *Admission*: 6-1-41; *Parent*: Mary; *Address:* Croydon Farm; *Home address*: 46, Springhead Rd. Erith, Kent ; *Last school*: Crescent Road School; Cause for leaving: Returned to Kent.

Josephine Hopkins: *Born*: 1-5-36; *Admission*: 22-4-41; *Parent*: Mary; *Address:* Croydon Farm; *Home address*: 46, Springhead Rd. Erith, Kent; *Cause for leaving*: Returned to Kent.

Raymond Bray: *Born*: 2-1-32; *Admission*: 3-3-41; *Parent*: Annie; *Address:* The Stores; *Home address*: 30, Brynmill, Swansea; *Cause for leaving:* Returned to Swansea.

Hilda Townsend: *Born*: 7-1-29; *Admission*: 7-4-41; *Parent*: Ernest; *Address*: c/o Mrs. Ford; *Home address*: 31 Cuff Crescent, Eltham; Readmitted after having been absent since 9-1941.

Doreen Morning: *Born*: 7-11-31; *Admission*: 22-4-41; *Address:* Stowey Farm; *Home address*: 16, Moxley Rd., Belevedere, Kent; *Cause for leaving:* Returned to Kent.

David Watson: *Born*: 11-1-30; *Admission*: 29-4-41; Address; c/o Mrs. J Baker; *Last school*: Bromborough Road, Birkenhead; *Home address*: 4, Eastern Ave., Port Causeway, New Ferry, Cheshire; *Cause for leaving:* Returned to Cheshire.

Jean Morgan: *Born*: 30-7-30; *Admission*: 9-6-41; *Parent*: James; *Address:* No. 5 Council Houses c/o Mrs. Hobbs; *Home address*: 10, Edward Str., Cardiff; *Last school:* Tredogarville Junior School; Cause for leaving: Returned to Cardiff.

Charles Parsons: *Born*: 30-9-33; *Admission*: 17-6-41; *Parent*: Joy; *Address:* Hart Cleeve Cottage c/o Mrs. Burridge; *Home address*: 68, Whitechurch Rd. Roath, Cardiff.

David Woolgrove: *Born*: 2-5-32; *Admission*: 2-9-41; *Parent:* Thomas; *Address:* The Bungalow, Knowle; *Last school*: Horsington Church of England School, Bath.

Brenda Hooten: *Born*: 2-11-32; *Admission*: 2-9-41; *Parent*: John; *Address:* Stowey Farm; *Home address:* 114, Molton Rd. Belvedere, Kent; *Cause for leaving:* Returned to St Augustine's School, Belvedere, Kent.

Peter Wilmore: *Born*: 8-4-35; *Admission*: 1-12-41; *Parent*: Harold; *Address:* Croydon Farm; *Home address*: 4, Charlesville Rd. Erith; Cause for leaving: Returned home.

Derek Morgan: *Born*: 9-12-32; *Admission*: 29-6-42; *Address:* 1 The Bungalow, Knowle; *Last school*: Horsington Church of England School, Bath.

Gwendoline Tregidgo: *Born*: 23-6-31; *Admission*: 7-9-42; *Parent*: William; *Address:* Croydon Farm; *Last school*: Otterhampton Church of England School; *Home address*: 55, Belgrave Rd. Plaistow E 13.

Pamela Tregidgo: *Born*: 8-10-33; *Admission*: 7-9-42; *Parent*: William; *Address:* Croydon Farm; *Last school*: Otterhampton Church of England School; *Home address*: 55, Belgrave Rd. Plaistow E13.

Alwyn Tregidgo: *Born*: 18-12-35; *Admission*: 7-9-42; *Parent*: William; *Address:* Croydon Farm; Last *school*: Otterhampton Church of England School; *Home address*: 55, Belgrave Rd. Plaistow E13.

Sheila Pauline Pring: *Born*: 1-33; *Home address*: Bristol, Avon.

Anthony R (Tony) Pring: *Born*: 1-35; *Home address*: Bristol, Avon.

Philip Burton: *Born*: 1-2-36; *Admission*: 7-9-42; *Parent*: Frank; *Address:* Coombe Cottage c/o E Coles; *Last school*: Marlpool Heanor, Nottinghamshre; *Home address*: 24, Westfield Ave. Heanor, Nottinghamshire.

Philip Rexworthy: *Born*: 16-8-37; *Admission*: 8-2-43; *Address:* (1) Great House Cottage c/o Mrs Richards (2) The Stores, c/o Mrs Delbridge.

Edward Schofield: *Born*: 8-2-38; *Admission*: 23-3-43; *Address:* The Stores c/o Mrs. Delbridge; *Last school*: Hagh Road Rothwell; *Home address*: 33, Haigh Rd, Rothwell, Leeds.

David Finch: *Born*: 26-3-38; *Admission*: 5-7-43; *Address:* Kitswall c/o Clifford Needs; Cause for leaving: Evacuated to Bath Nov 1940.

John Beckett: *Born*: 13-4-38; *Admission*: 16-9-43; *Address:* Post Office c/o Mrs Webber; *Last school;* Washford Church of England School; *Home address*: Farm House Cottage, Washford.

Audrey Warre: *Born*: 29-10-31; *Admission*: 2-11-43; *Parent*: John; *Address:* The Police Station; *Last school:* Washford Church of England School; *Last address:* Washford.

Joyce Sealey: *Born*: 8-8-37; *Admission*: 1-11-43; *Address:* Council Houses c/o Mrs Baker: *Home address*: Market Street, Wooten Under Edge, Gloucester.

Kenneth Marshall: *Born*: 29-4-33; *Admission*: 21-2-44; *Parent*: Florence; *Address:* The Gardens c/o Mrs. Smith; *Last school*: Dulverton School; *Home address*: Ashwick House, Dulverton; *Home address:* 24, Brambley Rd. N Hammersmith W10.

George Patterson: *Born*: 25-9-33; *Admission*: 10-7-44; *Parent*: Arthur; *Address:* Knowle c/o Lady Ryder; *Last school*: Dorothy Barley Junior, Harold Road; *Home address*: 129, Davington Rd. Dagenham, Essex.

Ronald Patterson: *Born*: 26-5-35; *Admission*: 10-7-44; *Parent*: Arthur; *Address:* Knowle c/o Lady Ryder; *Last school:* Dorothy Barley Junior, Harold Road; *Home address*: 129, Davington Rd. Dagenham, Essex.

Sidney Patterson: *Born*: 26-6-37; *Admission*: 10-7-44 ; *Parent*: Arthur; *Address:* Knowle c/o Lady Ryder; *Last school*: Dorothy Barley Infants, Harold Road; *Home address*: 129, Davington Rd. Dagenham, Essex.

Maureen Jacobs: *Born*: 20-4-34; *Admission*: 11-7-44; *Address:* Rosemont; c/o Miss Cane; *Last school:* Norlington Road Junior, Leyton; *Home address*: 10 Windsor Rd. Leyton, E10.

John Michie: *Born*: 1-9-37; *Admission*: 12-7-44; *Parent*: John; *Last school*: Benylands College, Surbiton; *Home address*: 291, Surbiton Hill Park, Surbiton, Surrey.

Harold Suttle: *Born*: 21-7-32; *Admission*: 13-7-44; *Parent*: George; *Last school:* Hazelrigge Road; *Home address*: 395A Clapham Rd London SW.

Eric Kidby: *Born*: 28-3-31; *Admission*: 7-7-44; *Parent*: Walter; *Address:* 6 Council Houses c/o Mrs Bircham; *Last school*: Dunraven Sn Streatham SW 16; *Home address*: 97, Mount Earl Gardens, Streatham SW16.

David Burry: *Born*: 9-9-34; *Admission*: 17-7-44; *Parent*: David; *Address:* The Old Mill c/o Fred and Edith Ray; *Last school*: Cormont Road Brixham, SW9; *Home address*: 4, Baldwin Crescent Camberwell SE.

Alan Few: *Born*: 15-2-38; *Admission*: 18-7-44; *Address:* Council House c/o Mrs. Clatworthy; *Home address*: 159, Adare Walk, Streatham SW16; *Last school*: Heathfield Road Streatham SW 16.

Joan Betty Wombell: *Born*: 27-8-35; *Admission* 5-9-44; *Parent*: Mrs. Nelly Wombell; *Address:* Knowle c/o Lady Ryder ; *Last school:* Star Junior School; *Cause for leaving*: flying bombs; *Home address*: 13, Homefield Gardens Mitcham, Surrey.

Diana Bennett: *Born*: 15-5-39; *Admission*: 5-9-44; *Parent*: Mrs. Ethel Bennett; *Address:* (1) Brook House (2) Knowle. *Last school:* Mariest Convent Tottenham L.C.C.; *Home address*: 176, Northumberland Park Tottenham N17; *Cause for leaving:* flying bombs.

Charles T. Mehegan: *Born*: 4-10-33; *Admission*: 5-9-44; *Parent*: Leslie Mehegan; *Address:* No. 6 Council Houses c/o Mrs. Bircham; *Last school*: Eglinton Road Woolwich; *Home address*: 139, Eglinton Rd Plumstead S.E.18; *Cause for leaving*: returned home, 25-6-45.

James K. Mehegan: *Born*: 23-9-36; *Admission*: 5-9-44; *Parent*: Leslie Mehegan; *Address:* No 6 Council Houses c/o Mrs. Bircham; *Last school*: Eglinton Rd. Woolwich; *Home address*: 139, Eglinton Rd. Plumstead S.E. 18; *Cause for leaving*: returned home, 25-6-45.

Ernest Edward Cattle: *Born*: 27-11-40; *Admission*: 5-9-45; *Parent*: Ernest; *Cause for leaving*: Removed to Reading.

Harvey Ernest Place: *Born*: 22-2-41; *Admission*: 5-9-45; *Parent*: John Baker Place; *Address:* Beasley; Last school: St Teresa's, Minehead. Cause for leaving: Removed to Reading.

Frank Reynolds: *Born*: 14-7-35; *Admission*: 8-10-45; *Parent*: Horace Reynolds; *Address:* Croydon Farm; *Last school*: Combe Florey Junior; *Cause for leaving*: Removed to Combe Florey.

Ralph Reynolds: *Born*: 11-5-37; *Admission*: 8-10-45; *Parent*: Horace Reynolds; *Address:* Croydon Farm; Combe Florey Junior; *Cause for leaving:* Removed to Combe Florey.

Samuel Reynolds: *Born*: 27-11-40; *Admission*: 8-10-45; *Parent*: Horace Reynolds; *Address:* Croydon Farm; Last school: Combe Florey Junior; *Cause for leaving:* Removed to Combe Florey.

Elsie Reynolds: *Born*: 19-11-40; *Admission*: 26-11-45; *Parent*: Horace Reynolds; *Address*: Croydon Farm; *Last school*: Coombe Florey; *Cause for leaving*: Removed to Combe Florey.

David Milne : *Born*: 4-11-35; *Admission*: 5-11-45; *Parent*: Alexander Milne; *Address:* South Lodge Knowle; *Home address*: Wooton nr. Dorking; *Cause for leaving*: Removed to Taunton 7-48.

Alfred John Robinson: *Born*: 14-10-37; *Admission*: 2-9-46; *Parent*: RC Robinson; *Address:* The Old Forge; *Home address*: East Walton, Norfolk.

Betty Florence Robinson: *Born*:15-6-41; *Admission*: 2-9-46; *Parent*: RC Robinson; *Address:* The Old Forge; *Home address*: East Walton, Norfolk.

Irene Myfanwy Wood: *Born*: 23-9-40; *Admission*: 21-5-46; *Parent*: Charles Wood; *Address:* Croydon Farm; *Cause for leaving:* Removed to Reading, 27-7-48.

Frederick Hinkley: *Born*: 28-1-34; *Admission*: 21-5-46; *Address:* Croydon Farm; *Home address*: Queens Rd Wimbledon; *Cause for leaving*: Removed to Frome, 6-12-46.

Daphne Ambrose Gilliams: *Born*: 30-11-35; *Admission*: 8-9-47; *Parent*: Edward; *Last school:* Attended Wootten Courtenay School first; *Home address*: Albert Road, Romford.

Douglas Lewcock: *Born*: 19-8-40; *Admission*: 9-9-47; *Parent*: Frederick; *Address:* c/o Mrs Jury; *Last school:* Attended Wootten Courtenay School before transfer to Timberscombe; Cause for leaving: Returned to Romford, 19-9-47.

Francis May Biss: *Born*: 12-5-43; *Admission*: 31-5-48; *Parent*: John; *Address:* Ford Cottages c/o Mrs Dyer; Home address: Hunniwins Farm, North Molton.

Audrey Jane Ward: *Born*: 13-5-36; *Admission*: 28-6-48; *Parent*: Henry William Ward; *Address*: No.3 Willow Bank; *Home address*: Earl Lane, Wembley; Cause for leaving: Removed to Bletchley, 19-6-48.

Brian William Ward: *Born*: 16-5-41; *Admission*: 28-6-48; *Parent*: Henry William Ward; *Address:* No. 3 Willow Bank; Last school: Sudbury Junior; *Cause for leaving*: Removed to Bletchley, 19-6-48.

Kathleen Irene Hales: *Born*: 8-4-43; *Admission*: 6-9-48; *Parent*: Wm Hales; *Address:* No. 3 Willow Bank; *Last school:* Blagdon Hill Junior; *Cause for leaving*: Removed to Shropshire, 6-4-48.

Roger Reginald Robinson: *Born*: 10-10-43; *Admission*: 27-9- 48; *Parent*: R Robinson; *Address:* 9 Willow Bank; *Home address*: Hitcham, King's Lyn.

James Richard Jenkinson: *Born*: 28-5-39; *Admission*: 4-10-48; *Parent*: S Jenkinson; *Address:* The Bungalow. *Last school*: Attended Wootten Courtney School before transfer to Timberscombe; Last school: Haywood Boys; *Cause for leaving*: Removed to Hitcham King's Lyn, 14-3-49.

William John Millard: *Born*: 9-1-44; *Admission*: 6-1-49; *Address:* Police Station; *Cause for leaving*: Removed to Bruton.

David John Dorning Ashton: *Born*: 16-9-39; *Admission*: 2-5-49; *Parent*: Wh Ashton; *Address*: Rose Cottage, Luccombe; Cause for leaving: Removed to Exeter.

Judith Iona Door: *Born*: 13-9-43; *Admission*: 3-6-49; *Address:* Beasley Farm; *Cause for leaving*: Removed to Sherborne.

Michael Thomas: *Born*: 13-9-43; *Admission*: 6-3-49; *Address:* Mrs. Badcock, The Gardens; *Home address*: 155 Acton Lane, Cheswick; *Cause for leaving*: removed 19-6-53.

Judith Mary Perkins: *Born*: 22-2-41; *Admission*: 5-1-50; *Parent*: Gordon J. Perkins; *Address:* The Stores; *Home address*: Shirley, Surry.

Margaret Louise Perkins: *Born*: 14-5-44; *Admission*: 5-1-50; *Parent*: Gordon J Perkins; *Address:* The Stores; *Home address*: Shirley, Surry.

Gillian Judith Ireland: *Born*: 10-9-42; *Admission*: 23-10-50; *Address*: Knowle; *Last school*: Attended Wooten Courtney School before transfer to Timberscombe School.

Shirley Margaret Brown: *Born*: 13-2-43; *Admission*: 3-3-52; *Parent*: Robert Brown; *Address:* The Vicarage, Timberscombe.

Robert William Brown: *Born*: 15-9-44; *Admission*: 25-3-52; *Parent*: Robert Brown; *Address*: The Vicarage, Timberscombe.

Timberscombe School Teaching Staff During the War

Teachers listed here appear in the 1939 Populaton Register. From Mrs Willis's journal, we know a number of other teachers were appointed during the war years. Sometimes they stayed less than a week. In addition to her other duties, Mrs Willis had the constant task of requesting replacement teachers from the County Education Committee and supervising them.

Head School Mistress: **Kathleen Annie (Axon) Willis** was born 25-6-1904 in Minehead. She and her husband, **William Henry Willis** (1902-14-3-1962), married in 1934 in Williton and were living in Tiverton when she was appointed head mistress of the Timberscombe School (11-10-1935). She died 7-7-1984 in Minehead.

Amelia Mary Land, who was born 18-5-1907, was appointed on 31-8-1937. She lived at Ford Cottage.

Sybil M Mould, who was born 14-9-1909, was evacuated from Bristol on 21-5-1941. She taught at the Timberscombe School until 13-12-1944.

Two teachers lived at Knapp with Frederick Cockram, a retired farmer, and his wife Edith. They were **Emily Annie King**, born 15-10-83, and **Ailsa M E Lines**, born 19-9-10. Miss Lines came to Timberscombe with the evacuees from West Ham, Essex. She taught the infants.

Two schoolmasters from West Ham lived at Wreford, Wootten Courtenay. **Frederick George Hadlow**, who was born 26-2-1909, and **Benjamin J Spink**, who was born 8-10-09. Both men were thirty.

The LCC (London County Council) also sent **Francis G. Holland** (born 19-5-12) to teach evacuee students. He lived on Marlett Road in Minehead.

Above: Newly arrived evacuees (September 1939)
(courtesy of St. Petrock's History Group)

ACKNOWLEDGEMENTS

My interest in the children and mothers evacuated to Timberscombe during World War II began several years ago with anecdotes told to me by older villagers. Then Angie Gummer rescued old Timberscombe School documents from the rubbish bin, including the school register and log book (1910-1947), and I became even more intrigued. I set out hoping to find some of these people. I couldn't have proceeded with my search without assistance from The Somerset Heritage Centre; Minehead Museum; and St Petrock's History Group's photographic archives and Oral History Project.

Grateful acknowledgment to AM Heath Literary Agency for permission to use excerpts from *Little Legs: Muscleman of Soho* by George Tremlett. Invaluable sources include:1939 Population Register - National Archives; Records and minutes from the Somerset County Council Education Committee; The WVS/WRVS Narrative reports - Royal Voluntary Service, Williton Rural District 1939-1941 (Royal Voluntary Service 1939-2016); *'Send Them to Safety'*, by James Roffey (2009, Evacuation Reunion Association); *Away and Home – World War II,* by Patricia Herniman (2016, Papermill Books, The Little Baddow History Centre); *Exmoor Village,* by Hilary Binding and Brian Pearce (2004, Exmoor Books); *Memoirs of Selworthy and West Somerset,* by Cicely Elaine Cooper (1951, Cox, Sons and Co. Ltd); *Exmoor in Wartime* 1939-1945, by Jack Hurley (1978, The Exmoor Press); *Exmoor Village,* WJ Turner, ed. Photos by John Hinde (1947, Harrap & Co. Mass Observation Archives Trust, University of Sussex); *No Time to Wave Goodbye,* by Ben Wicks (1989, St Martin's Press); *Little Legs: Muscleman of Soho, by* George Tremlett (1989, HarperCollins); "Problems of Social Policy", *History on the Second World War, United Kingdom Civil Series,* Edited by K. Hancock and Richard M. Titmuss (1950, HMSO).

I wish to thank those individuals whose contributions have made this book possible, particularly former evacuees who shared their personal stories and photographs: Jacqueline Gande Nunney, Eddie Gande, Ernie Munson, John Munson, Thomas Robinson, Maurice Huxtable, James Lambert, Norman Sutton, Charles Mehegan and John Gratton. Few are still around who can relate first-hand accounts of those years, and I'm grateful to each of them for their time and generosity. I'm indebted to Helen Tompson for her suggestions and advice and also to Anne Stamford for making the book better with her keen eye for detail. And finally, thank you to the following for sharing their remarkable memories and research: Robert Hart, Margaret Reed, Marion Fewless, Joy Booth, Archie Dyer, Peter Nesbitt, Angie Gummer, Joyce Smith, Mary Holcombe, Reg Holcombe, Gwynie Poole, Marion Jeffrey, Tom Sperling, and Jeff Cox.